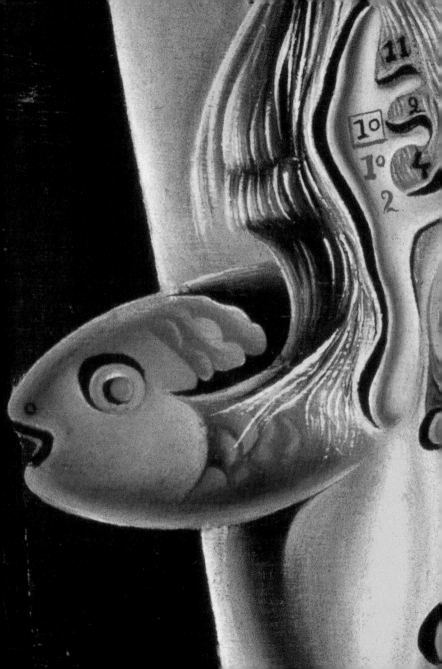

CONTENTS

1 A CATALAN CHILDHOOD
12

2 DALI, LORCA AND BUNUEL
20

3 PARANOIAC EXPERIENCE VERSUS AUTOMATISM
44

4 FROM THE GREAT MASTURBATOR TO THE MYTH OF NARCISSUS
70

5 THE WORLD AND ITS DESIGNS: FROM OBJECT TO ARCHITECTURE
90

6 AVIDA DOLLARS RETURNS TO ORDER
110

Documents
129

Index
156

DALÍ
THE IMPRESARIO OF SURREALISM

Jean-Louis Gaillemin

Dalí was born into a Catalan family of notables and intellectuals, with many musicians and painters in its circle of friends. Barcelona, with Gaudí's Parc Güell and Sagrada Familia, formed his first aesthetic impressions. This was the environment that spurred him on to become an artist.

CHAPTER 1

A CATALAN CHILDHOOD

When he was 16, Dalí, right, registered at the School of Drawing in Figueras. He loved to lose himself in nature and wanted to be an Impressionist – a desire that can be seen clearly in *Portrait of My Father* (c. 1921), left, which depicts the irascible notary from Figueras against the bay of Cadaqués in the light of the setting sun. Dalí was determined to take courses at the Academy in Madrid and pursue his studies in Rome.

On 11 May 1904, nine months and ten days after the death of an older brother named Salvador Galo Anselmo Dalí, Salvador Felipe Jacinto Dalí was born, and this Salvador was the one we have all heard of. Charming, temperamental, imperious, capricious, pampered, loved, spoilt by three women – his mother, grandmother and elder sister – not to mention countless maids, young Salvador tyrannized his adoring family, under the authority of a dominant father whom he never opposed until he was twenty-five.

A Catalan childhood

This was above all a Catalan family, from Barcelona and Figueras, a large market town in the fertile plain of Ampurdán. Being Catalan meant fighting for a federal Spain and the Catalan language; it also meant

The Dalís lived inland but spent their summers in a little house in Cadaqués, beside Es Llané beach. Taken from the terrace, this family portrait (*c.* 1910), above, shows from left to right: Aunt María Teresa, Dalí's mother and father, Salvador, Aunt Catalina, sister Ana María and grandmother Ana. The Pichots, who were friends of Pablo Picasso (1881–1973), lived nearby.

a certain internationalism, thanks to the rich and busy seaport of Barcelona, which imported its wealth from Cuba and distributed it primarily to the Catalan people. Being Catalan and a Dalí meant being liberal-minded and cultivating an anticlericalism tinged with socialism. And it meant undying love for and loyalty to France, particularly Paris, as the First World War would later confirm. With its modern architecture, thriving galleries of contemporary art, bookshops (one of which was owned by Salvador's maternal uncle, Anselm Domènech) and numerous concert halls and theatres, Barcelona was a flourishing international arts centre.

The Dalís lived in Figueras, a short distance from the French border at the foot of the Pyrenees. On market days, the town was invaded by peasants from the surrounding countryside, and on Sundays it put on the airs and graces of a big city while the town band played Pietro Mascagni's (1863–1945) *Cavalleria Rusticana*. During the winter holidays, the Dalís would visit the Barcelona branch of the family, in particular Uncle Domènech's bookshop, and take walks in Parc Güell, which architect Antoni Gaudí (1852–1926) had begun in 1900.

Inspired by nature

During the summer the family would go to the port of Cadaqués, on a barely accessible peninsula, where the ancient vineyards had been ruined by phylloxera and the land had been painfully converted for fishing. This ecological disaster gave the landscape its mineral look, harsh and austere, and the terraces that had been created for the vines lent even greater severity to the arid slopes of the hills. To round off this extraordinary setting, Cape Creus – Spain's most easterly point – is formed by schistose mica rocks that have been eaten away and sculpted by the tramontana in 'a grandiose geological delirium', to use the words of Dalí himself. He was fascinated by these polymorphous monsters, with their ability to turn from cock to camel to anvil to female breasts. One of these rocks, like a face leaning on its nose, was to become *The Great Masturbator* (1929), a key image in the 1930s.

Salvador, below, was a pampered child, dressed up like a doll. His father, a freethinker, sent him to the local school, which had a lasting effect on the future megalomaniac: 'Indeed I became more and more used to considering myself, a rich child, as something precious, delicate, and absolutely different from all the ragged children who surrounded me…. I alone had hair that was combed a thousand times and that smelt…of a perfume….' (*The Secret Life*)

The Pichots, a family of gifted artists, were among Dalí's neighbours in Cadaqués. Picasso and his lover Fernande Olivier came to visit the patriarch of the family, Pepito Pichot, in 1910.

Paranoiac awakening

Salvador was sent by his radical father to a lay primary school. The head, a moody man named Trayter, introduced him to the mysteries of magic-lantern projections, but he much preferred to create his own images, as he did at Cape Creus: 'In the course of my interminable and exhausting reveries, my eyes would untiringly follow the vague irregularities of these mouldy silhouettes and I saw rising from the chaos which was as formless as clouds progressively concrete images which by degrees became endowed with an increasingly precise, detailed and realistic personality.' (*The Secret Life*) In 1916 he entered the local secondary school in order to pursue his studies in Castilian, and he also attended the school of the Marist Brothers, as they taught in French. In addition, he registered for evening classes at the Municipal School of Drawing, on Pepito Pichot's advice.

Right up to date

The first articles that Dalí published in *Studium* (a magazine that he collaborated on with a group of his friends between January and June 1919) show him indulging in passionate analysis of the great masters. His typography and illustrations were Viennese in style, but his earliest canvases were Impressionist. 'I always

This *View of Cadaqués* (1920), left, was painted by Dalí from Poal beach. Cadaqués is in the middle of a peninsula, cut off from the mainland by its bay and Mediterranean creeks. Dalí would return here throughout his life to draw inspiration from the landscape that had formed his first aesthetic emotions: 'Each hill, each rocky contour might have been drawn by Leonardo himself…with the lines formed by the retaining walls that terraced the vines accentuating and shading [the soil], having esthetically the function of geodetic lines marking, giving emphasis and architectonic compass to the splendor of that shore, which seems to descend in multiple and irregular stairways adapted to the soil….' (*The Secret Life*) This architectonic feature was glorified by the painter in 1925, and Cadaqués was celebrated for the plenitude and rich precision of its lines.

Right: Photographs of Cape Creus. During the 1930s, the tortured landscape of the coastal areas excited Dalí's imagination. One crumbling rock, like a face leaning on its nose (above), was to give rise to a key image: *The Great Masturbator*.

admire the great French Impressionists – Manet, Degas, Renoir. I hope they will guide me firmly along the way. I have changed my technique, my range is much clearer,' he wrote to Uncle Anselm, who sent him the reviews *Valori Plastici* and *L'Esprit Nouveau*. Pepito Pichot introduced him to the Futurists and the French Cubists. Salvador divided his time between country walks, strolls around town, and decorous flirtations with fellow student Carme Roger. Dalí's father did nothing to encourage these developments, however. On the grand piano in the living room, he displayed a medical book with vivid colour illustrations of venereal diseases.

Between aesthetics and politics

Dalí's notebooks reveal a political awareness that was even more focused than that of his father. He avidly followed the course of the civil war in Russia and earnestly called for a revolution in Catalonia: 'Then the time of terrorism will come, days of darkness, mass executions.… But this time it will be the turn of the humble and the oppressed, mad and fanatical, to give vent to their thirst for justice and hatred in the bloody streets of Barcelona.… Trotsky has prophesied that Spain will follow the Russian example.…'

With faith in his career as an artist, in May 1920 Salvador was looking forward to the coming summer: 'It was as though I was already painting, and I was carried away, quite carried away thinking about the joyous day when, after a year of demands, emotions and lies, I could begin the conscious work, the sacred work, of the creator.… More light, more blue…more sun…losing myself in Nature, being her submissive disciple.… Oh I could go mad!' (*The Shameful Life of Salvador Dalí* by Ian Gibson) Ramón Pichot (1872–1925) lent him his studio in a dilapidated fisherman's shack, and the following winter he took over an abandoned house in Figueras. In the meantime, he assumed the persona of the artist, with his long

.TROTSKY.

Dalí's *Self-Portrait with Raphaelesque Neck* (*c.* 1920–21), left: 'I had let my hair grow as long as a girl's, and looking at myself in the mirror I would often adopt the pose and the melancholy look which so fascinated me in Raphael's self-portrait, and whom I should have liked to resemble as much as possible. I was also waiting impatiently for the down on my face to grow, so that I could shave and have long side-whiskers. As soon as possible I wanted to make myself "look unusual", to compose a masterpiece with my head; often I would run into my mother's room – very fast so as not to be caught by surprise – and hurriedly powder my face, after which I would exaggeratedly darken the area around my eyes with a pencil. Out in the street I would bite my lips very hard to make them as red as possible....' (*The Secret Life*) In another self-portrait, a pipe (which Dalí did not smoke) and a hat with a large brim completed the image of the 'anarchist artist'.

hair, floppy necktie, and a felt hat that he had specially ordered, which was designed to be unfashionable. His successes in 1922 softened the blow of his mother's death (in 1921) to a certain extent: a joint exhibition was held in January by the Association of Catalan Students at the Dalmau Gallery, and a few months later the same gallery staged a Francis Picabia (1879–1953) exhibition, which was presented by French poet André Breton (1896–1966) in person. Their paths were to cross again seven years later in Paris.

The picture of *Trotsky* (*c.* 1923), far left, reflects this period of ardent revolution.

Dalí met Federico García Lorca and Luis Buñuel in Madrid, both of whom were to play a pivotal role in his artistic evolution. With Lorca, he developed a Purist aesthetic under the 'patronage' of Saint Sebastian, while Buñuel drew him into the adventure of *Un Chien Andalou* and introduced him to the Parisian Surrealists.

CHAPTER 2
DALI, LORCA AND BUNUEL

The *Barcelonese Mannequin* (1927), left, first exhibited at the Dalmau Gallery in Barcelona, mixes pure aesthetics with personal fantasies, such as the fish floating in the thigh. The two interlocking heads would subsequently turn into those of Dalí and Lorca, photographed, right, in Cadaqués by Ana María, Dalí's sister, in 1925.

The intellectual environment in Madrid was completely different. Dalí had lodgings in the Residencia de Estudiantes, a student hostel that was based on the English model and housed nearly one hundred and fifty students from different faculties and institutions of higher education. The 'Resi', a liberal establishment independent of the State and Church, had no chapel and its library subscribed to international journals. H. G. Wells, Albert Einstein, Paul Valéry and Max Jacob all gave lectures there. In April 1925, the poet Louis Aragon (1897–1982) delivered a brilliant piece of Surrealist provocation: 'Ah! Bankers, students, workers, officials, servants, you are the fellators of the useful, the wankers of necessity…. And first of all, we shall ruin this civilization which you hold so dear…. Western world, you are sentenced to death.'

Dalí conscientiously followed courses at the Special School of Painting, Sculpture and Engraving in Madrid, which was part of the Royal Academy of Fine Arts. In the evening he shut himself in his room, and he devoted his Sundays to visiting the Prado. The shyness and eccentricity of this boy from the provinces used to bring a smile to the faces of the Anglo-Saxon dandies at the

The student card for 1924–25 (above) at the Special School of Painting, Sculpture and Engraving shows a long-haired Dalí with the floppy necktie of an 'artist'. In the class photo (below), Dalí is sitting bottom left, and a fellow student is pulling his hair. After his expulsion in 1923 for disorderly behaviour and his imprisonment under the dictatorship of Primo de Rivera, Dalí had become a star, waging open rebellion against the professors for whomImpressionism was still an aesthetic yardstick.

'Resi'. Pepín Bello recalled how the artist often blushed and seemed completely indifferent to the female of the species. According to Dalí, Bello was the first person to bring him out of his shell: 'One day when I was out, the chamber maid had left my door open, and Pepín Bello happening to pass by saw my two cubist paintings. He could not wait to divulge this discovery to the members of the group. They knew me by sight, and I was even the butt of their caustic humor. They called me "the musician", or "the artist", or "the Pole"....' (*The Secret Life*)

The Ultraists

The dominant figure in this group was Luis Buñuel (1900–83), born in Aragon and nicknamed 'Tarquin the Superb' because of his fine physique, his sporting prowess, and his exploits in Madrid's brothels. At that time he was trying to make his way in the natural sciences and was pursuing the ideas of the 'Ultra', a group of artists who advocated a militant Modernism in the wake of Purism and Futurism. Their intellectual leaders were Guillermo de Torre and Rámon Gómez de la Serna, a friend of Tristan Tzara (1896–1963) and Picasso, who launched the fashion for *greguerías* (concise, Dadaist metaphors).

Having heard that an old-fashioned romantic had dared to declaim some work by French Symbolist poet Paul Verlaine (1844–96), Guillermo de Torre interrupted a meeting by shouting: '"Universal hatred of the moon!" says Marinetti [Futurist poet Filippo Tommaso Marinetti]. What's this I've just heard? A snatch of Verlaine? Unworthy sons of 1923! What has it served you to be born beaneath the wings of aircraft? And you still dare to call yourself avant-gardists, when you don't even know that the combustion engine sounds better than any hendecasyllable?' (*The Shameful Life of Salvador Dalí*) Dalí was won over, adopted their hairstyle, and learned to do the Charleston during their nocturnal sorties to the bars of the old city.

The picture above, *Nightwalking Dreams* (1922), evokes the nocturnal escapades of Dalí and his 'Ultraist' friends: the Uruguayan painter Rafael Pérez Barradas (1890–1929) and Luis Buñuel, with his mighty shoulders. Leaning on Dalí, who is identifiable by his long hair and arched eyebrows, is Maruja Mallo, a girl from the school. The picture recalls Madrid in the 'years of debauchery', which Dalí describes self-indulgently in his memoirs: 'It was five o'clock, and the last minute was approaching.... With a sense of bitterness we uncorked a fresh bottle of champagne. My friends' eyes were moist with tears.' (*The Secret Life*)

The beginnings of a friendship

Dalí's 'Cubism' was extremely eclectic. The influence of Juan Gris (1887–1927) and Giorgio Morandi (1890–1964), with additional touches of 'Vibrationism' and 'Planism' – avant-garde movements in Barcelona – are to be seen in the fragmented self-portraits, in which he also inserted newspaper collages (*L'Humanité*, to which he subscribed, and *La Publicitat*) as well as urban elements. The night scenes add an Expressionist note to these shattered figures. It was at this point in Dalí's life that Federico García Lorca (1898–1936) made his entry. A published poet and excellent musician, he had a charm and vivacity that gave him star quality, even if some people were put off by his homosexuality, which his more indulgent acquaintances called his 'flaw'. The arrival of this star from Granada made the bright lights of the Ultraists seem dim by comparison: '…the personality of Federico García Lorca produced an immense impression upon me. The poetic phenomenon in its entirety and "in the raw" presented itself before me suddenly in flesh and bone, confused, blood-red, viscous and sublime, quivering with a thousand fires of darkness and of subterranean biology, like all matter endowed with the originality of its own form.' (*The Secret Life*)

Dalí and Lorca had a burning artistic ambition, sexual frustration and a caustic sense of humour in common, but these similarities led to a clashing of characters. Indeed, according to Dalí, the first stage of his life in Madrid was marked by the violent antagonism between Lorca's extremely religious (erotic) spirit and Dalí's own

The picture below, *Portrait of Federico García Lorca* (1923), was painted in his room at the Residencia, and bears witness to the shared artistic tastes and close friendship of Dalí and Lorca.

Right: *Self-portrait with L'Humanité* (1923).

Far right: Among the group photographed at the Residencia, Lorca and Dalí are at the front, wearing light-coloured jackets.

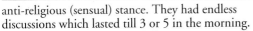

anti-religious (sensual) stance. They had endless discussions which lasted till 3 or 5 in the morning.

Within a year, Dalí was a different man. An unjust expulsion, coupled with a period of imprisonment at the start of Primo de Rivera's dictatorship, gave him hero status on his return to the 'Resi' in September 1924. He was increasingly attracted to Lorca: 'I avoided Lorca and the group, which grew to be his group more and more. This was the culminating moment of his irresistible personal influence – and the only moment in my life when I thought I glimpsed the torture that envy can be. Sometimes we would be walking, the whole group of us, along El Paseo de la Castellana on our way to the café where we held our usual lierary meetings, and where I knew

Lorca would shine like a mad and fiery diamond. Suddenly I would set off at a run, and no one would see me for three days.' (*The Shameful Life of Salvador Dalí*)

Perhaps there was also an element of fear of a passion which he equated with that of Maldoror, the hero of the poet Comte de Lautréamont's (Isidore Ducasse, 1846–80) *Chants de Maldoror*. Dalí must have been struck, like the Parisian Surrealists, by the character of Merwyn, the youth whose beauty Lautréamont compares to 'the chance meeting on a dissection table between a sewing machine and an umbrella', and who is the object of Maldoror's passionate and murderous affection. Dalí could not help but draw parallels with Lorca: 'The Shadow of Maldoror hovered over my life, and it was just at this period that for the duration of an eclipse precisely another shadow, that of Federico García Lorca, came and darkened the virginal originality of my spirit and of my flesh.' (*The Secret Life*) Dalí was not insensitive to the attentions of the poet, even if fear prevented him from responding to them. It was an erotic and tragic love because it could not be shared, Dalí told his biographer Ian Gibson three years before his death.

The relationship was strengthened during the Easter holidays (1925), when the poet was invited to Cadaqués and captivated the Dalí family. Federico, himself under the spell of Dalí, invited his friend to join him in Andalusia for the summer, but Dalí turned him down because he wanted to keep to the September deadline for his first exhibition at the Dalmau Gallery.

Under the sign of Purism

Madrid Cubism, an ephemeral homage to the avant-garde, was followed by a 'return to order', in keeping with the vacations and periods Dalí spent in Cadaqués.

Painted in 1924, *Port Alguer*, above, depicts Cadaqués. Its simplified, geometrical houses suggest a Cubism tempered by the Neo-Classicism seen by Dalí in the Italian review *Valori Plastici*. In the foreground are the curved figures of women carrying pots, a feature of many contemporary pictures in which homage to Catalan women was intertwined with local traditions and festivals. In 1925, Lorca stayed in Cadaqués for the first time and charmed the whole Dalí family with his recitations, improvisations and piano-playing. It was during long walks at Cape Creus that the poet learned about the painter's 'paranoiac' vision (see Chapter 3).

The 1924 still lifes are bathed in the cold light and shade characteristic of Morandi. One of them, entitled *Purist Still Life*, is a homage to the formal eurhythmy of the Purists Le Corbusier (1887–1965) and Amédée Ozenfant (1886–1966). The figures installed among these clearly defined shadows have the rigidity of Giorgio de Chirico's (1888–1978) tailors' dummies. A view

This *Still Life* of 1924, above, subtitled *Siphon and Bottle of Rum*, with its hollowed-out bottle, its geometrical slice of watermelon, and its interlocking boxes and frames, mixes a Cubism inspired by the Juan Gris of the 1910s with the still lifes of Carlo Carrà (1881–1966) and Giorgio Morandi. 'The musical construction of the painting expresses a limpid precision and a triumphant harmony,' wrote one Madrid critic in *Buen Humour*. Dalí gave it to Lorca in 1927, as can be seen from the photo (left) of the poet in his bedroom.

of the port of Cadaqués, *Port Alguer* (1924), shows this tendency towards a colder, more geometrical vision, in which the Mediterranean sun beats down mercilessly on the solid shapes of the white houses.

Within two years, this return to order was completed with drawings in the style of Jean-Auguste-Dominique Ingres (1780–1867) and the heavily structured portraits of his sister, which are set against a geometrical and architectural background. These are characterized by an almost brutal Realism, although it is countered by certain subtle details. In the frontal portrait of Ana María at Cadaqués, *Portrait of a Girl in a Landscape (Cadaqués)* (*c.* 1926), her impassive expression is in effect undermined by a certain anatomical inconsistency: the flat *décolleté* reveals a total absence of bosom, whereas the dress itself is full of strange and disturbing protuberances. In *Girl Standing at the Window* (1925), the solid curves of Ana María are seen from the back, inviting us to contemplate a natural calmness. The room's bare walls frame the window, through which the quiet ocean is visible with its sculpted, clearly defined waves 'that one can count'. Nothing disturbs this intimate vision, apart from a crumpled cloth on the window sill. At the same time Dalí was painting weighty figures in large

This *Self-Portrait* of 1926, below, with 'arched eyebrows and detached ears' is reminiscent of other composite heads, some of which represent Lorca and Dalí.

Below left: Salvador and Ana María, photographed in the mid-1920s.

Right: *Venus and Sailor* (1925).

compositions, for example *Venus and Sailor* (1925), where the figures take on a monumental form against the cheerful background of the port with its ships and their pennants.

The 'Ode to Salvador Dalí'

On 11 April 1926, Dalí took the train to Paris, accompanied by his aunt and sister, where they were met by Buñuel and Manuel Angeles Ortiz (1895–1984), a friend of Lorca's who introduced Dalí to Picasso in his studio on the rue de la Boétie. 'I've come to see you before visiting the Louvre,' said Dalí, somewhat intimidated. 'You're quite right,' replied Picasso, and then proceeded to show him his latest works – still lifes and large, Neo-Classical figures.

The Dalís went to Brussels next, where Salvador was able to gaze at the work of two of his heroes: Hieronymus Bosch (1450–1516) and Johannes Vermeer (1632–75). On his return, Dalí found the 'Ode to Salvador Dalí' in the *Revista de Occidente* – one hundred and thirty lines in which passion, disguised as aesthetics, pleads its case: 'O Salvador Dalí, with your olive voice / I do not praise your imperfect adolescent brush… / But I hail your longing for eternal limits.' The sense of limitation, of geometry, of 'material defined and exact', of the 'straight line' and the 'learned crystals [that] sing their geometries' is set under the aegis of 'Minerva, the constructor of scaffolds'.

Shortly afterwards Lorca sought to consummate his passion. He was accompanied by Margarita Manso, a student at the Beaux-Arts and a free spirit with the body of a boy, who was very attached to the two friends.

Overleaf: Two portraits of Ana María. Left: *Girl from the Back* (1925). The girl's body is framed by the geometrical structure of the houses, with a roof echoing the line of her shoulders. The rungs of the chair merge ambiguously with the low wall in the background. Right: *Portrait of a Girl in a Landscape (Cadaqués)* (*c.* 1926). The frontal view is thrown off balance by the extraordinary diagonal which drastically distorts the dress.

When Dalí rejected his advances, Lorca made love to Margarita right in front of him. 'Having failed to get me to put my arse at his disposal, he swore to me that the sacrifice obtained from the girl was balanced by his own sacrifice of himself: it was the first time he had made love to a woman.' Dalí, still a virgin, took no part in the frolics.

Saint Sebastian, patron of objectivity

On his return to Spain in 1926, Dalí organized his departure from Madrid by getting himself expelled. He returned to Cadaqués and announced a response to the 'Ode' under the aegis of Saint Sebastian, the patron saint of modern artists. As Dalí himself pointed out to Federico – reminding him in a letter that representations of the martyr never made any suggestion that arrows pierced his behind – this patronage is not without sexual allusions. At the beginning of March he returned to the subject: 'In my "Saint Sebastian" I think of you a lot and sometimes I think it's you….' (*The Shameful Life of Salvador Dalí*)

In Dalí's article, which finally appeared in July, Saint Sebastian is described as a mixed being, of nickel and plaster, of blood and humours, half machine and half organism. Dalí's magnifying glass enables him to see 'a succession of vivid sights perceived in a necessary order of measures and proportions': a girl without breasts, sailors dancing the Black Bottom on white liners, female polo players reflected in the nickel-plated headlights of the Isotta Fraschini, a chloroformed bistoury in a shop window 'lying stretched out fast asleep like a Sleeping Beauty'. These mechanical, cinematographical, eurhythmic visions with traces of Man Ray (1890–1976), Buster Keaton, de Chirico, Morandi and Le Corbusier were

Saint Sebastian, patron saint of pictorial objectivity according to Dalí and Lorca, is omnipresent in their work. He is celebrated by Dalí in a text of 1927, illustrated by *Saint Sebastian with the Head of a Sole*, below, one of the nicknames affectionately bestowed on Lorca by Dalí. With this painful celebration of the mutilated body,

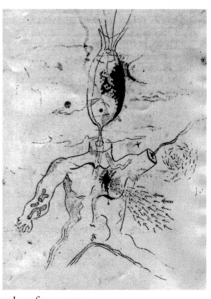

Dalí was referring in word and image to an icon of the modern artist, illustrated before him by French painter Odilon Redon (1840–1916).

there to be recorded by the artist, a modern Sebastian. In reply to Lorca, Dalí takes refuge in a sanitized world where emotions and the body are contained within prostheses. But how long will they remain there?

For a year the composite head of Dalí and Lorca put its signature to various clearly defined compositions following the Sebastian theme, such as *Composition with Three Figures: Neo-Cubist Academy* (1926): Saint Sebastian as a sailor, naked beneath his cap, standing at an equidistance from the sculptured forms of a lewd Venus and a wise Minerva. In the foreground is the double head of Lorca and Dalí, symbolizing their friendship (which is echoed by the two crossed fish-ties).

After a summer at Cadaqués, Lorca replied, saying that Dalí's marble Saint Sebastian was opposed to his

Closing the cycle of *Venus and Sailor* paintings, *Composition with Three Figures: Neo-Cubist Academy*, above, was finished in 1926. It illustrates the illusory indifference of a Saint Sebastian between the two figures of Sensuality and Science. The two interlocking heads of Dalí and Lorca, like the two fish-ties in the foreground, equate this apparent impassiveness with an impossible love.

own, who was made of flesh and died every moment. If Lorca's Saint Sebastian were too plastic, he would not be a lyrical poet, he added. Here Sebastian confirms rather than heralds an aesthetics under threat.

Indeed, it was not long before these little theatres of harmony began to fill up with curious pieces of 'apparatus' – geometrical bodies, stiff or flexible, mounted on clumsy stilts and streaked with veins or splashed with blood. They seem to have a tottering life of their own. They swarm all over *The Forest of Apparatus* and *Apparatus and Hand* (1927), in which the rocky construction in the foreground is threatened by a cyclone and is surrounded by

mutilated, decomposing or gestating bodies. From its top, covered in eurhythmic veins and blood, there emerges a red hand, swollen and trembling – the hideous manifestation of one final convulsion. *Little Ashes* (1928) illustrates the fall of these great, monumental bodies that decompose and burst into a welter of breasts, vaginas, fingers, torsos dripping with blood, pieces of apparatus and bodies merging and changing under the hallucinatory eye of the painter.

Scarcely had it taken on the mantle of theory when sanitized eurhythmy found itself overwhelmed by life, death and sex. During the summer of 1927, at Cadaqués, Lorca joined in the celebration of the

With *Apparatus and Hand* (1927), above, the sanitized world of Saint Sebastian begins to wobble under pressure from the unconscious. Buffeted by a whirlwind bearing phantasms, the 'apparatus' trembles on its rickety crutches, while a turgescent hand rises frenetically from its top, and the earth is covered in putrefaction.

autonomy of the little things: 'Think of me when you are on the beach, and especially when you are painting the little ashes unique and crackling – ouch, my little ashes!…and kiss me…' he wrote on his way home.

These amorphous organisms and little things began to intertwine beneath the white light of the beaches:

The putrefaction and disintegration of bodies in *Apparatus and Hand* reaches its climax in *Little Ashes*, overleaf. It is continued in pictures such as *The Spectral Cow* (1928),

spectral cows and rotting donkeys, male and female bathers distorted by *Unsatisfied Desires* (1928), a picture that caused a scandal in Barcelona. Hands and fingers cross or are clenched across space.

Towards the end of 1928 this tension is relaxed in abstractions that seem to float over the empty canvas. Dalí appears to have come to an impasse, and this Minimalist reduction is accompanied by a growing interest in photography and the cinema.

above, or *The Putrefied Donkey* (1928), where all that remains of the body is an unlikely collection of organic matter proliferating or fading away on antediluvian shores.

Buñuel and the cinema

It was at this point that Luis Buñuel stepped in. He was jealous of the friendship between Dalí and Lorca, whose

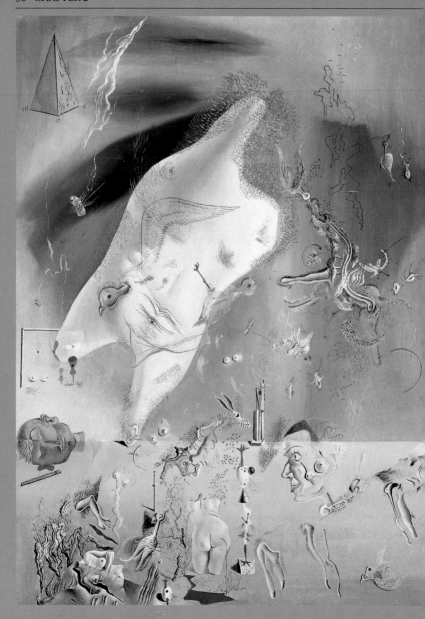

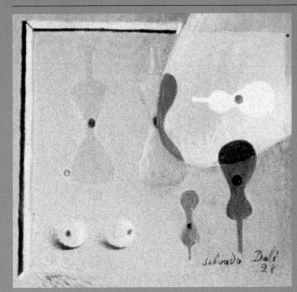

Far left: *Little Ashes* (1928) is a manifesto. By signing on the dislocated frame of a Purist composition, Dalí was declaring an explosive end to the eurhythmic, sanitized world of Saint Sebastian. Abandoning the Cubist guitars to their sterile game, the two balls become the breasts and the pink oval the stump of a torso (detail, above right). Under the staring eye of the painter (detail, below right) modelled on Lautréamont's Maldoror, the face pitted with forms of delirium and the neck gripped by the teeth of two donkeys, the 'little things' are freed in a whirl of emancipation: genital hands, pendulum hands, 'solitary' breasts, an isolated thumb, spectral donkeys. On the ground, as immobile as pieces of a puzzle, are breasts held up by smoke, a torso pissing blood, an apparatus made of bird's feet, geometrical objects, ambiguous organisms, crazy machines. The gigantic torso staggers along, threatened on all sides by putrefaction, and seems to be in danger of crashing and exploding. An 'apparatus' taken over from de Chirico's mannequins stands untouched on the horizon.

The pictures of *The Bather* (*Man Bathing*, above left) and *The Bather* (*Woman Bathing*, below left), both from 1928, denote the condition of human 'architecture' after the revolution that began with *Apparatus and Hand* and ended with *Little Ashes*: the figures are indistinct, fragmented, mutilated, in a state of decomposition or gestation. The male bather, reduced to an obscene big toe, is surrounded by threads of flesh that are either escaping or coming together. To the right of this amorphous mass, covered with red and blue veins, a Medusan vortex floats above the water. Further away, in the sea, the body of a phantasmic woman has detached itself from a shell-like rock which is as jagged as the waves: this is the monstrous birth of Venus (detail, above right). Another Olympian parody: stuck to her rock, the female bather evokes the fantastical consciousness of the hysterical body, with each limb assuming the importance given to it by the unconscious: indistinct genitals, the tiny head of a carnivorous insect, masturbating hand, turgescent breast (detail, below right), anamorphic body.

Left: *Four Fishermen's Wives of Cadaqués* (1928) shows Dalí's inability to transplant desires onto the structured anatomy of objectivity. These symbolic reductions go to the very limits of abstraction.

The sculpture *Anthropomorphic Beach* (1928), below, refines its erotic allusions to the point of primitivism.

homosexuality disgusted this macho *bon viveur*. From Paris he wrote to their mutual friend Pepín Bello: 'Federico sticks in my crow incredibly.... His extreme narcissism was already enough to make a pure friendship with him impossible.... Dalí is deeply under his influence. He believes himself to be a genius, thanks to the love Federico professes for him.... How I'd love to see him arrive here and renew himself far from the influence of the nefarious García! Because, and it's a fact, Dalí is a real male and very talented!' (*The Shameful Life of Salvador Dalí*) This attempt to make contact came at just the right time. The publication of *Romancero Gitano* prompted a long letter from Dalí to Lorca, in which protestations of friendship scarcely conceal an aesthetic clash. In it, Dalí tells Lorca that his present poetry falls completely into the category of traditional poetry; and although Dalí can detect the most magnificent poetic substance ever seen, it still sticks entirely to the norms of conventional poetry. For the first time, Dalí invokes Surrealism. His final compliment sounds, with hindsight, like a farewell: 'Goodbye. I believe in your inspiration, in your astronomic fatality.'

During his four years in Paris, Buñuel had hardly moved beyond the world of the *métèques* (wogs), as the colony of artists in Montparnasse were then called. Writing film reviews had brought him closer to the cinema, but he was only a part-time journalist. His sympathy for the Surrealists did not stop him from viewing Man Ray's work as too 'full of *esprit*'. His ideal, like that of Dalí, was a popular 'anti-artistic' cinema, above all American. He thought that 'the pure Surrealist film, the dream-like scenario' was itself a concession to art. The models were Harry Langdon, the sad clown, or Adolph Menjou, the 'Parisian' seducer with the eloquent moustache. For Dalí the cinema represented a way of realizing the metamorphosis of objects that were so laborious to paint. He wanted to 'liberate the little things' on the wider canvas of the silver screen. His ideal was to adapt the conventions of the documentary and the mélodrama to produce an 'objective record of reality'. He did not want to seek formal or sensational effects, but to trap reality by subverting the stereotypes of narrative as he had done in his 'little proses', keeping the framework of the picaresque tale in order to give a better account of the adventures of a 'slice of roast beef'.

In January 1929, the two of them were back in Cadaqués to write a script. Working with questions and immediate answers, they said whatever came into their heads and wrote it down together. Thus were formed the links between 'strings, slabs of cork, Marist Brothers, grand painos and rotting donkeys' in a scene of

In this *Portrait of Luis Buñuel* (1924), below, painted during Dalí's period of Purism, the square-shouldered figure of Luis Buñuel – against a geometrical suburban background – conveys the powerful character of the man. He was extremely jealous of the friendship between Dalí and Lorca, and never ceased to complain about the 'harmful' influence of the latter. Buñuel suggested that he and Dalí collaborate on a film scenario, which eventually became *Un Chien Andalou (An Andalusian Dog)* – a title that could refer to Lorca himself.

attempted rape, for example. 'In fact we caused an explosion of irrational images, with no explanation,' said Buñuel. Many of these images sprang from a background common to students from the 'Resi', while others were already present in the work of Dalí (the eye and the razor, the sea urchin, the ant-covered hand) or Buñuel. Some were also taken from Lorca, like the effeminate cyclist based on his *El Paseo de Buster Keaton* (*Buster Keaton's Outing*), or his reappearance on the bed, alluding to the poet's staging of his own death. The anti-hero full of anguish against the heroine's bosom, but ecstatic when faced with her buttocks – might this be Lorca himself, the *chien andalou* (Andalusian dog), as contemporary students at the 'Resi' used to call those who came from southern Spain?

First successes in Paris

Shooting began at Billancourt in early April, with Dalí playing one of the two Marist Brothers in the rape scene. The film had its premiere on 6 June at the Studio des Ursulines, together with *Les Mystères du Château de Dé*, which the collector and arts patron Charles de Noailles had commissioned from Man Ray. The latter suffered by comparison, and a dazzling audience – including Picasso, Le Corbusier, Jean Cocteau, Christian Bérard, Fernand Léger, Tristan Tzara and the entire group of the Surrealists – gave *Un Chien Andalou* an ovation. Buñuel, who had filled his pockets with stones, did not need to use them.

In December, Dalí and Buñuel appeared in *La Révolution Surréaliste* as part of a photo collage containing fifteen apostles grouped around Breton. The same edition contained reproductions of two recent pictures: *Illumined Pleasures* (1929) and *Accommodations of Desire* (1929). In six months Dalí had become a Surrealist painter.

The grand piano, augmented by two 'Marist Brothers' and a rotten donkey, was an obsession shared by Dalí and Buñuel. The hero drags it along painfully, signalizing his impotence. It reappears in *William Tell*, a major work from 1930, as a symbol of frustrated desire. After finishing *Un Chien Andalou* (two images below) in 1929, Dalí and Buñuel, left, returned to Cadaqués for the summer.

Despite his contact with the Surrealists, Dalí did not renounce his 'objective' aesthetics. The intransigence of this 'new Rimbaud' – bolstered by the power of the vision he christened 'paranoiac' – owed a great deal to the liberating influence of Gala Eluard.

CHAPTER 3

PARANOIAC EXPERIENCE VERSUS AUTOMATISM

In this photo, right, of Dalí at Cadaqués, Gala Eluard is superimposed, as the woman who retrospectively gives the artist new life. The little group of Surrealists that had assembled at Cadaqués got her to ask Dalí if the man with the soiled underpants in the foreground of *The Lugubrious Game* (1929), left, reflected a coprophilous streak in the painter.

Dalí first came into contact with Surrealism through *La Révolution Surréaliste*, founded in 1924. The review introduced him to Joan Miró's (1893–1983) *The Hunter* and *The Ploughed Field* (both 1923–24) and Yves Tanguy's (1900–55) *The Ring of Invisibility* and *Lost Animals*. It is possible to find traces of and allusions to all these canvases in his *Little Ashes*. They encouraged Dalí to liberate the 'little things', clustered together in the unreal organisms which were themselves influenced by the exploding structures of André Masson (1896–1987). Years later Dalí boasted that he pinched everything from 'Uncle Yves', but the role model remained Miró, lionized during his time in Paris.

Encouragement from Miró

In October 1927, Miró, on the recommendation of the critic Sebastià Gasch, visited Dalí at Cadaqués, accompanied by Parisian businessman Pierre Loeb. In a letter to Gasch, Dalí described their visit as brief and said that Miró's personality impressed him a great deal, although they hardly spoke a word. What interested the two visitors most were the last two canvases – *The Forest of Apparatus* and *Apparatus and Hand* – which they found to be reminiscent of Yves Tanguy but superior, more natural and infinitely more plastic in technique. Dalí conveyed his enthusiasm to Lorca and praised the stark purity of Miró, who 'paints children with hairs, genitals etc.'. Miró's pantheistic eroticism and his fantastical anatomies exacerbated Dalí's 'unsatisfied desires' and helped him to overcome his reservations regarding Surrealist automatism. In fact, there was nothing more contrary to his vision of objectivity than the unrestricted licence for the unconscious that was advocated by the *Manifeste du Surréalisme* (André Breton's first *Surrealist Manifesto* of 1924). In *The New Limits of Painting*, Dalí preferred to quote Breton's *Le Surréalisme et la Peinture* (1928), where he found a link between the 'autonomy' that Breton gave to objects and words, and the 'emancipation of little things' which formed the foundation of his 'objectivity'. Breton sought to refute the positivist theory of the 'subliminal memory', and insisted on the importance of the self in the creative process. But the 'great subjective light' of

In *Illumined Pleasures* (1929), above, Dalí covers the canvas – already filled with various boxes – with the new figurative elements that were engendered by the experience of *Un Chien Andalou*. The indeterminate objects include a shell, the head of the Great Masturbator, self-portrait as a jug joined to a bust of his sister,

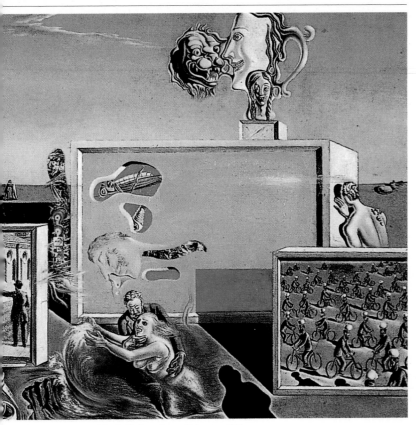

the artist was a black light, that of doubt: 'There are no landscapes. Not even the horizon. There is, on the physical side, nothing but our immense suspicion which envelops everything.' Only the self allows us to escape from the void.

The surreal contained in the real

For Dalí, this irrational concept of creation legitimized 'the necessary absence of cohesion' that permeates his work. Taking over the Bretonian 'doubt', he declared that the artist's role was to systematize the confusion of the real by imposing his individual truth, where 'the purest subconscious' was in operation. According

and a peeping Tom. The bearded man supporting the voluptuous lady is reminiscent of Sigmund Freud (1856–1939). Here Dalí is taking up an iconographic tradition characteristic of Surrealism, beginning with de Chirico's *Child's Brain* (1914) and continued by Max Ernst in *Revolution by Night* (1923).

to Breton, this anchorage in the self was accompanied by an adherence to reality which, again to Dalí's great satisfaction, expressed 'a philosophy of immanence': 'Everything I love, everything that I think and feel, inclines me toward a special philosophy of immanence, according to which surreality would be embodied in the very reality and would not be superior or exterior to it.' (Haim Finkelstein's *The Collected Writings of Salvador Dalí*) This 'infra-reality' allowed Dalí to accept automatism, as we can see from this passage about Miró: 'Joan Miró's paintings lead us, by a route of automatism and surreality, to come nearer to appraising and verifying reality itself, thus fully corroborating André Breton's thoughts, according to which surreality would be contained in reality and vice versa.' In *Réalité et Surréalité*, the Bretonian formula provided Dalí with a guarantee that automatism was no longer a matter of 'listening' to the dictates of the unconscious, but was a direct transformation of the 'targeted' given. The process here was the automatic 'conversion' of reality, and the revelation of its incoherence under the arbitrary gaze of the self. It was what in 1930 Dalí christened the 'paranoiac experience'.

Paris is ours

With the shooting of *Un Chien Andalou* in spring 1929 and his simultaneous submission of some 'purely documentary' articles on Paris to the review *La Publicitat*, Dalí was able to try out this Surrealism. For instance, in a café on the Champs-Elysées: '"There are" eighteen buttons, the one closest to me has a hair (perhaps an eyelash or a tiger's hair) coming out of one of its holes. Three centimeters to the right of this button there is a cookie crumb.... Beyond the crumbs and continuing to the right there is a dark abyss two hand-spans in width. On the other side of the abyss "there is" a table hanging on a thin and long wisp of smoke.... Suddenly the

In *The Hand* (1930), below, the giant hand, deformed by desire, shows the offensive activity that feeds the fantasies at the back of the central figure. He is stained with blood that spurts from the antique column, and his own excrement is soiling the volute on which he is seated. Dalí has given prominence to the Art Nouveau character of this eclectic ornament, in order to bring out a degree of relaxation in the face of these impulses.

following things take place in a very rapid succession: seven hands follow one another, three gloves are introduced in three hands, two hands leap on top of a chair, one on top of a table three meters away…. At this moment, the hands, gloves, buttons, hair, etc. are substituted by the avenue of Champs-Élysées that still glows in the afternoon light. The avenue disappears to be replaced by the window of a shoe store, lighted up electrically from the inside….' (*The Collected Writings of Salvador Dalí*)

Dalí's stay in Paris was enriched by many encounters. Miró made him wear a dinner jacket, took him to various salons, and introduced him to Camille

Paul Eluard (above, on the left) met Dalí in Paris during the filming of *Un Chien Andalou* in April 1929. That summer he visited Dalí with Gala, and his later correspondence with her reveals an admiration and loyalty which led him years later (in 1934) to vote against the proposal by André Breton (above, on the right) to expel Dalí from the Surrealists. Breton, who was as impressed by Dalí's paintings as by his writings, called him a new Arthur Rimbaud (1854–91) and bought a number of his canvases, including *Accommodations of Desire* and *William Tell*, which reflects the father-son relationship that both of them acknowledged.

Goemans, who was exhibiting some collages by Picasso, Jean (Hans) Arp (1887–1966), Ernst and René Magritte (1898–1967) in the rue de Seine. Goemans responded immediately, signing an exclusive contract for an exhibition at the end of the year. Dalí was enthusiastic about Man Ray; he visited his studio and was given a viewing of his film *Les Mystères du Château de Dé*. Goemans introduced him to Magritte as well as to Paul Eluard, who took him to various nightclubs. The ultra-shy virgin from the provinces was mortified by all the temptations of Paris, and when he returned to his hotel, his head pounded with images from the day: 'And coming back to my immeasurably prosaic hotel room, my legs aching with fatigue from my fruitless comings and goings, I felt the bitterness of frustration fill my heart. Mortification at not having been able to attain the inaccessible beings whom I had grazed with my glance filled with imagination. With my hand, before my wardrobe mirror, I accomplished the rhythmic and solitary sacrifice in which I was going to prolong as much as possible the incipient pleasure looked foward to and contained in all the feminine forms I had looked at longingly that afternoon, whose images, now commanded by the magic of my gesture, reappeared one after another by turn, coming by force to show me of themselves what I had desired in each one! At the end of a long, exhausting and mortal fifteen minutes, having reached the limit of my strength, I wrenched out the ultimate pleasure with all the animal force of my clenched hand, a pleasure mingled as always with the bitter and burning release of tears….' (*The Secret Life*) At the end of Dalí's stay, Eluard, Magritte and Goemans promised to come and see him that summer in Cadaqués.

A polymorphous eroticism

The erotic shock of Paris and his experience of the cinema gave new impetus to the eye of the painter. Beneath the gaze of the infant Dalí, symbolizing his return to the naive view that precedes language, *The First Days of Spring* (1929) celebrates the renewal of a world of crude collages and colour prints, of unsophisticated figures and vulgar allusions. The

Right: *The First Days of Spring* (1929) signals a renaissance. Dalí's return to a conventional perspective creates the new abstract and neutral space that will encompass his future work. Figures return, but schematically, sometimes in the form of collages or enhanced transfers: the little girl, the bearded man, or the men in suits accompanied by highly eroticized women-objects. Two pictures-within-a-picture evince a desire to escape both from abstraction (on the right, painted with irregular surfaces in six different colours) and from the eurhythmic vision of Purist aesthetics (on the left, a framed colour print showing the bridge of an ocean liner). Beneath the gaze of the infant Dalí are many features of the paintings to come: the Art Nouveau ornament, the face-jug with savage teeth, the head of the Great Masturbator, and a giant grasshopper. Beyond the vision of the baby are a little girl and a bearded man, two well-dressed men riding an ornamental socle, a man sitting on a chair with his back turned to the scene, and on the horizon a father and child.

This detail of *The First Days of Spring*, left, shows an ambiguous couple. A woman in grey tights is sitting on a socle. Her vagina is hidden but is denoted by the thick red slash of the cravat. Her face has been replaced by an indeterminate anatomical orifice, from which a swarm of midges is escaping. Beneath her top we can see two bulging breasts. A man in a suit kneels beside her, his mouth gagged, his head leaning against her neck, his hands over a bucket and forming multicoloured curves that represent an anus and a vagina.

phallic shadow of the little girl holding out a purse
to a Freudian old man, the homosexual couple, the man
with the vaginal hands, the diaphanous, necrotic head
that will later become *The Great Masturbator* – all evince
the naive jollity of gingerbread men.

The Lugubrious Game (see p. 44) accentuates the swirl
of fantasies in a huge mirage extending before the
outsize hand of an androgynous creature that is hiding
its face. In the foreground is a male couple (father and
son?) spattered with blood and excrement, their pose
ambivalent. Above the head of the masturbator (whose
eyes are closed), the erotic imagery takes on a double
form: a woman's breast becomes the testicle beneath a
phallic finger. Rabbits' ears or the brims of hats, bearded
mouth or cigarette smoke – everything serves to imitate
the slit of the vagina, while the blood-stained buttocks
are also objects of desire. The presence of a chalice and
Host adds the spice of blasphemy to the obscenities.

Despite their admiration, the visitors found it difficult
to conceal their misgivings, particularly about the man
with soiled underpants. It was Paul Eluard's wife Gala
who was given the task of expressing their concerns.

Breton thought
*Accommodations
of Desire* (1929), above,
was prophetic: 'With
Dalí it is perhaps the
first time that our
mental windows have
opened completely and
that we are going to feel
ourselves slipping
towards the trapdoor
to the fulvous sky....
Dalí's art, the most
hallucinatory that has
been produced up
to now, constitutes
a veritable threat.
Absolutely new
creatures, visibly
mal-intentioned, are
suddenly on the move.'
(*The Shameful Life of
Salvador Dalí*)

Accommodations of Desire, another picture dating from 1929, seems rather more refined: around a homosexual couple (father and son?) who are devouring each other, figures of desire are projected onto boulders, seeming to signify either terror or masturbation. In the top right-hand corner a lion replaces a vagina on the trunk of a female body full of strange eruptions, and beside it are hairy orifices and an insinuating hand. Elsewhere the ambivalent manes of big cats signify dangerous and unknown territory, and a swarm of ants scurries in or out of what looks like a vagina. Desires or fears? There are sharp teeth everywhere. Nothing on this desolate shore of dangerous rocks suggests sexuality at ease with itself.

Enter Gala Eluard

Gala Eluard entered Dalí's life in 1929. She was Russian, born into a family of government officials in Kazan, had learned to read French with the Comtesse de Ségur, and had continued her studies in a private institution because, at that time, girls were not allowed to go to university. While at a sanatorium in Switzerland, she had met Eugène Grindel, later to become Paul Eluard. Their marriage and the birth of a daughter did not prevent the couple from living sexually liberated lives. Max Ernst, whom they met in Cologne, formed a *ménage à trois* with them when

Photograph of the Surrealist group, taken by Man Ray in 1930. From left to right: Tristan Tzara, Paul Eluard, André Breton, Jean Arp, Salvador Dalí, Yves Tanguy, Max Ernst, René Crevel and Man Ray himself. Looking rather cramped in his suit, Dalí is still the slender, shy boy but he would very soon become aware of his own talents as an artist and theorist at the very centre of the group, and also as a provocative but charming star in the worldly circle of his first collectors and patrons. He came onto the scene at just the right time, replacing André Masson as the leading painter, and it did not take long for him to arouse the envy of Max Ernst.

he came to Paris, and he painted her in *The Rendez-Vous of Friends* (1922), with her back turned to the group of Surrealists, showing her independence. Nicknamed '*la Tour*' or '*la Sybille des steppes*' by the Surrealists, Gala dragged Eluard into an orgy of sex, as we learn from the poet's letters: 'Last night there was a great band of moonlight in the room, and I saw you, really saw you,

completely naked with your legs spread wide, and you were being taken by two men, in the mouth and in the vagina. And you were brown and very beautiful. And even now, when I recall it, I think that for me you are the incarnation of love, the most intense incarnation of desire and erotic pleasure.'

Gala was ten years older than Dalí, but she was the embodiment of all his childhood dreams of a little Russian girl: 'It was she! Galuchka Rediviva! I had just recognized her by her bare back. Her body still had the complexion of a child's. Her shoulder blades and the sub-renal muscles had that somewhat sudden athletic tension of an adolescent's. But the small of her back, on the other hand, was extremely feminine and pronounced, and served as an infinitely svelte hyphen between the willful, energetic and proud leanness of her torso and her very delicate buttocks which the exaggerated slenderness of her waist enhanced and rendered greatly more desirable. How had I been able to spend the whole previous day with her without recognizing her, without suspecting anything?' (*The Secret Life*) Juvenile, androgynous, callipygous, she inspired confidence with her thirty-five years. The impact was immediate. 'Overnight, Dalí was a changed man,' wrote Buñuel, who had come to Cadaqués to work on a new film script. 'He did nothing but repeat whatever Gala said

Left: *Portrait of Gala* (1931).

Below: Photograph from 1929, showing Dalí (on the left) and Paul Eluard (on the right).

Right: *Portrait of Paul Eluard* (1929) reveals the sympathy between the two men. Eluard, who impressed Dalí with his elegance and relaxed manner with women, is here surrounded by various new features in Dalí's imagery. Perhaps Eluard had also used his wife's charm to ingratiate himself with the artist.

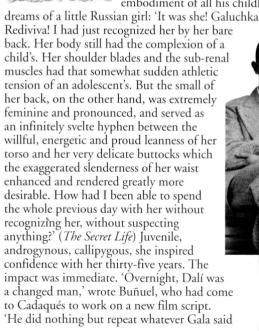

– a complete transformation.' Did they have the tacit approval of Eluard, who had commissioned Dalí to do his portrait, and who sometimes used his wife to lay his hands on artists' works behind the backs of their dealers? Was the decision that of a woman seduced or calculating? At the end of the allotted period, Gala stayed behind in Cadaqués, to the great annoyance of Buñuel and to the fury of Dalí's father, who looked askance at his son's liaison with a married woman right in front of his daughter. Dalí panicked: 'Never in my life had I yet "made love", and I represented this act to myself as terribly violent and disproportionate to my physical vigor – this was not for me.' (*The Secret Life*) And indeed the idyll seemed to be going nowhere. Vows and confidences ended up in promises: Gala would wait

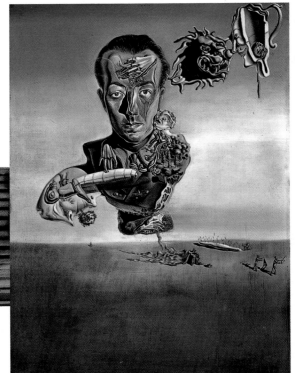

Overleaf: Two photographs taken at Port Lligat (in 1931) in the little fisherman's shack which Dalí bought in 1930 thanks to an advance from Charles de Noailles, one of his first patrons. Originally a simple hut, it was transformed and extended over a period of more than fifty years. In front of a limewashed wall, where a stone table brought the guests together during the summer, we see the head of Dalí. He is playing one of the optical games which he was fond of incorporating in his 1938 pictures (*Invisible Afghan with Apparition of García Lorca's Face on the Beach in the Form of a Fruit Bowl with Three Figs*), his head appearing to be part of the meal laid out on the table. In the neighbouring olive grove, Dalí has erected a perspectival pair of simple columns with flat capitals, and during the summer of 1931 he took a series of photographs here with Gala and René Crevel playing 'walk-on parts'. (It was during this stay that Crevel wrote *Dalí, ou, l'Anti-Obscurantisme*, the first study of Dalí's paintings and writings.) These columns are to be seen again in *The Invisible Man* (1929–33), and the mysterious drapes recur in *William Tell*, illuminated by the light of the setting sun.

for Paris and Dalí's first exhibition in order to play her part as the instructor. But she left with several pictures, including *The Lugubrious Game* and the *Portrait of Paul Eluard* (1929).

Breton salutes the new Rimbaud

Presented by Eluard, the latest work caused a stir and, even before the exhibition at Goemans Gallery, Charles de Noailles and Breton bought *The Lugubrious Game* and *Accommodations of Desire* respectively. At this time the Surrealist group was experiencing a crisis. Michel Leiris, Georges Limbour and other dissidents had gathered round Georges Bataille, who, with the support of Georges Wildenstein, had founded the journal *Documents*. *La Révolution Surréaliste*, on the other hand, had folded in 1929 through lack of funds. Breton embarked on the *Second Manifeste du Surréalisme* (*Second Surrealist Manifesto*),

Pictured below is *The Enigma of Desire, My Mother, My Mother, My Mother* (1929) (detail, above, and full picture, below). Inside the cavities, over and over again, is the inscription 'ma mere'.

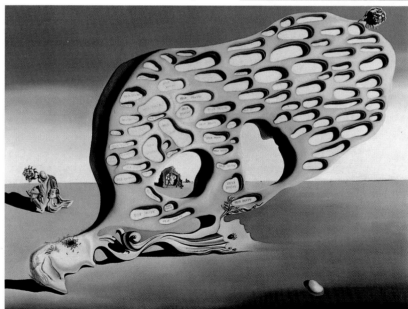

in laborious, vindictive prose full of declarations of intent and accounts being settled.

Basking in the glory of *Un Chien Andalou*, Dalí played the part of the wild card. In the preface to the Goemans catalogue, Breton rediscovered the tones of a Verlaine welcoming a Rimbaud who must be protected against the vermin (Georges Bataille and his gang), which wanted to batten on. 'With Dalí it is perhaps the first time that our mental windows have opened completely and that we are going to feel ourselves slipping towards the trapdoor to the fulvous sky....' (*The Shameful Life of Salvador Dalí*) Breton savours these fears in an apocalyptic tone: 'Dalí's art, the most hallucinatory that has been produced up to now, constitutes a veritable threat. Absolutely new creatures, visibly mal-intentioned, are suddenly on the move.' In the *Second Surrealist Manifesto*, which appeared in December, the great doctrinairian prophesied: 'It is to the innocence, to the anger of some men to come that it will fall to free from Surrealism that which cannot fail to live on, to restore it…to its proper goal.' The frontispiece of the second manifesto was entrusted to Dalí: the great masturbator, the woman-jug, lion head, keys, chalices and Hosts, and even excrement covered in flies, on the sides of a diamond – all constituted a rebus of his new mythology.

As far as devastation was concerned, Breton was to see it happen. In 1930, Dalí made a second film with Buñuel, *L'Age d'Or*, and it caused a scandal that revitalized the Surrealists, while his first article, 'The Rotten Donkey', confirmed his subversion of Bretonian automatism into the paranoiac experience.

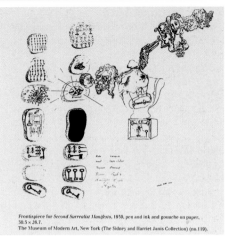

Frontispiece for *Second Surrealist Manifesto*, 1930, pen and ink and gouache on paper, 50.5 × 26.7.
The Museum of Modern Art, New York (The Sidney and Harriet Janis Collection) (no.119).

Breton entrusted Dalí with the task of illustrating the *Second Surrealist Manifesto* (frontispiece, above), thus showing his own advocacy of an art that was endowed with illuminating and prophetic power, as set out in his preface of 1929. In this text, Breton hopes that 'the admirable voice which is that of Dalí will not break…because certain "materialists" are interested in making him confuse it with the squeaking of his polished leather shoes.' Breton took over from Bataille, who had been the first to publish Dalí's work.

L'Age d'Or

L'Age d'Or marked an escalation in the degree of erotic provocation and sacrilege. 'Sometimes I take pleasure in spitting on the portrait of my mother,' Dalí wrote on one picture at the Goemans exhibition, much to the indignation of his widowed father. Driven out of the family home, he took refuge in Cadaqués with Buñuel to write the film script, which they finished in Paris in December. From a retreat on the Mediterranean, where he had gone with Gala, Dalí sent additional ideas to Buñuel, accompanied by illustrations. Certain sequences of dissolves, drawn with great precision, are reminiscent of the polymorphous fantasies in *The Lugubrious Game*. 'He looks at her, and we see her lips trembling…. Her face gently fades and her lips are subtly superimposed until one can see the actual lips of the depilated vagina, until these are indecipherable from the preceding lips.' One piece of dialogue was to create a furore: 'We must make the love dialogue seem as if they are speaking about something they already know. Her: "I have always desired the death of my children." Him: "My love". At this moment he can say: "My love" with his face covered in blood.' Buñuel modified some of the scenes. The heroine ripping off a fingernail with her teeth during a love scene was replaced by the caress of a mutilated hand. He later denied it but Dalí collaborated on the sacrilegious sequences, including a comparison between the sadeian Comte de Blangis and Christ.

Filmed in April 1930, *L'Age d'Or*, financed by Charles de Noailles, caused a scandal with its eroticism, scatology, blasphemy and scorn for the political world. The two images above are scenes from the film. The top image shows bishops (played by local fishermen) on the rocks at Cape Creus. The bottom image, filmed at Billancourt, sees the heroine sucking the toe of a statue.

The Rotten Donkey: the paranoiac conversion

At the same time, *Le Surréalisme au Service de la Révolution* (1930–33) appeared, in which the adjective

'paranoiac' was used for the first time to describe the active and sudden 'conversion' of reality triggered by unconscious desires. In 1928, Dalí had still believed that this visual 'conversion' could only take place by way of a 'distraction of passive character', but in 'The Rotten Donkey' he sees it as being active, in contrast to automatism: 'I believe the moment is drawing near when, by a thought process of a paranoiac and active character, it would be possible (simultaneously with automatism and other passive states) to systematize confusion and thereby contribute to a total discrediting of the world of reality.' (*The Collected Writings of Salvador Dalí*) Dalí insisted on the conceptual aspect of the paranoiac phenomenon – an interpretive

The picture above, *Profanation of the Host* (1929), shows the metastasis of a Great Masturbator whose head spits saliva and blood over a Host. In the left-hand corner, the Art Nouveau embellishments hidden in the shadows – symbolizing erotic perversions – mount their own assault on the chalice.

phenomenon which he contrasted with 'hallucination', a sensory phenomenon favoured by Carl Einstein in *Documents*: 'Standing wholly apart from the influence of the sensory phenomena with which hallucination is more or less taken to be associated, the paranoiac activity always makes use of materials that are controllable and recognizable…. Paranoia makes use of the external world in order to set off its obsessive idea, with the disturbing characteristic of verifying the reality of this idea for others. The reality of the external world serves as an illustration and proof, and is placed thus at the service of the reality of our mind.'

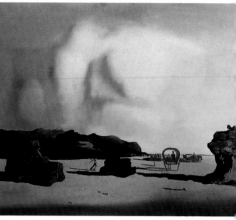

According to Dalí, the fundamental difference between targeted paranoia and spontaneous hallucination lies in the fact that the delirious paranoiac image contains nothing arbitrary and can be shared: '…the various forms assumed by the object in question will be controllable and recognizable by all, as soon as the paranoiac will simply indicate them.' Thus Dalí and Breton can read the same postcard of an African hut differently, seeing a woman's head and a portrait of the Marquis de Sade respectively.

This claim of communicability reveals a desire to escape from the 'madness' generated, and to legitimize all perversions: 'The new images, as a functional form of thought, will adopt the free disposition of desire while being violently repressed. The lethal activity of these new images, simultaneously with other Surrealist activities, may also contribute to the collapse of reality, to the benefit of everything which, through and beyond the base and abominable ideals of any kind, aesthetic, humanitarian, philosophical, and so on, brings us back to the clear sources of masturbation, of exhibitionism, of crime, and of love.' Far from viewing the paranoiac experience as a threat to the automatic processes, Breton

A point of transition, between 1931 and 1934, *Moment of Transition* (1934) stretches out into infinity, with its menacing rocks beneath enigmatic clouds in the evening light, creating a scene of mirages and hyperrealistic illusions. The top of a covered wagon merges with the dome of a town on the horizon, while the outline of the two wheels is reduced to two stakes stuck in the ground. The covered wagon was one of Dalí's obsessions for several years. In *Réalité et Surréalité* (1928), he used it to illustrate the 'sudden conversion of reality', prefiguring his theory of the paranoiac vision, published in 'The Rotten Donkey'.

gave his blessing to the enterprise, which seemed to him to crown his own efforts to synthesize Surrealism and Communism: '...dialectical thought combined with psychoanalytical thought, each crowning the other with what Dalí in such striking manner calls paranoiac-critical thought, [is] the most admirable instrument that has yet been proposed for driving into immortal ruins...the ever more attractive phantom of the future.'

Armed with this seal of approval, and drunk with gratitude to Gala, Dalí threw himself into his work.

These three pictures were juxtaposed and commented on by Dalí in a 'communication' published in *Le Surréalisme au Service de la Révolution* (1931) under the title *Paranoiac Face*: 'As a result of a study during which I had been obsessed by long contemplation of Picasso's faces, and particularly those of his black period, I was looking for an address in a pile of papers and was suddenly struck by the reproduction of a face which I thought was by Picasso – a face that was completely unknown. Suddenly, the face faded away and I realized it was an illusion.... Analysis of the paranoiac image in question enabled me, by way of a symbolic interpretation, to find all the ideas that had preceded the vision of the face. André Breton had interpreted this face as being that of de Sade, which linked up with a very particular preoccupation that Breton had with de Sade. In the hair of this face Breton could see a powdered wig, whereas I saw a fragment of unpainted canvas, as is often the case in Picasso's style.'

On the far left is *Wlliam Tell* (1930), which has given rise to many psychoanalytical commentaries. Dalí, who had recently been devouring some of Freud's major works, including *The Interpretation of Dreams*, did not hesitate to mix Freudian examples with his own symbolic creations – in the suspect light of biographical recollections. Thus new myths came into being, such as that of William Tell the castrator, armed here with a pair of scissors. The arrow shot by the Swiss hero at the apple-substitute is to be seen on the head of his son. The blood-stained scissors suggest that the sacrifice of the young man's manhood has already taken place.

In the image on the right, *The Font* (1930), on the marble floor of an archaic temple, a column with ornamental metastases, a soft stele with disturbing rebuses, an Art Nouveau woman-fountain gnawing her lips with lust, as in *The Dream* (1931) (p. 81), a woman-jug about to spit into a chalice, a fellating couple being spied on by a lion – all combine to make up a programme of perversions announced in the pages of *The Visible Woman*.

On the one hand, he systematized 'the confusion' of reality by introducing double images and anamorphoses, by contaminating genres and materials, by creating unreal spaces with contradictory shadows and ambiguous drapes. On the other hand, he developed the features of a personal mythology: the disgraced son, William Tell, the Great Masturbator, Gradiva. These characters, whose adventures and 'poses' were sketched out in drawings and poems, took on definitive forms in the great paintings. This was the time when a certain 'metaphysical' (in the de Chirico sense) fate imbued his crepuscular shorelines beneath protean clouds with the comforting unreality of metamorphoses: kleptomaniac phantoms, Adonises leaning on the shoulders of sympathetic rocks, young women for ever motionless beneath a light that never goes out. Time itself is abolished, conquered by the passive resistance of soft watches in *The Persistence of Memory* (1931). The canvas is an arena where images meet and depart, fighting for pre-eminence at the risk of being absorbed, of eventually disappearing themselves. So it was with *The Invisible Man* (1929–33), which Dalí spent four years 'not completing', the polymorphous perversity being more amenable to the scope and ambiguity of drawing (as can be seen from the frontispiece of *The Visible Woman*) than of painting.

Previous double page: The picture on the left is *Solitude* (1931), while that on the right is *Shades of Night Descending* (1931). For a short time in 1931, a calm, melancholy Dalí painted twilit beaches with figures draped in shrouds, concealing various objects. Delicate shells feed on the naked bodies, explaining their absorption into the surrounding rocks. With these pictures, Dalí came close to his Neo-Romantic friends, such as Christian Bérard and the Berman brothers.

Dalí's *The Great Masturbator* (1929), above right, is a self-portrait of Dalí sleeping on his fantasies, with a fellating woman – borrowed from a chromo – emerging from his neck. The phallic arum lily and the red tongue of the lion make the scene all the more explicit.

Perhaps Dalí's most famous painting, *The Persistence of Memory* (1931), below right, generally known as *Soft Watches*, was the result of an uncompleted picture (painted in the time it takes to watch a film), a splitting headache and a runny Camembert.

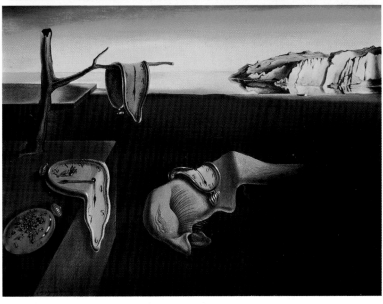

Having decided to 'systematize confusion', and encouraged by Jacques Lacan's thesis on paranoia, Dalí threw himself into 'the conquest of the irrational' in all domains. This conquest led to its own end through a narcissistic realization brought about by a new reality: Gala.

CHAPTER 4

FROM THE GREAT MASTURBATOR TO THE MYTH OF NARCISSUS

Painted in 1934, *The Spectre of Sex Appeal*, left, teeters before the horrified eyes of Dalí, dressed in a sailor suit and standing in one of the coves at Cape Creus. The sacks of potatoes, borrowed from Millet's *Angelus*, serve as orgasmic prostheses for a creature which despite its crutches looks as if it is about to collapse in one last mighty spasm.

Right: Photograph of Dalí, taken in 1930.

Support from Lacan

Among the readers of 'The Rotten Donkey' was a young psychiatrist, Jacques Lacan, who was working on the subject of paranoia. He visited Dalí and, two years later, the publication of his thesis *On Paranoid Psychosis and its Relation to the Personality* (1932) confirmed the artist's own intuition. For Dalí the delirium of interpretation was not an *a posteriori* process of reasoning designed to legitimize a false perception, but was inherent in the unconscious mental phenomenon of the work being perceived. Perception was in essence paranoiac, and vision was nothing but interpretation: 'Consideration of the paranoiac mechanism as a force and power operating at the very basis of the phenomenon of the personality, of its "homogeneous", "total" character, can only be confirmed in the most rigorous manner by reading Jacques Lacan's admirable thesis,' declared Dalí in the first issue of the review *Minotaure*. Lacan, a few pages later, explained that the paranoiac experience produced 'an original syntax' whose mechanism provided a remarkable mode of access to the 'symbolic values of art and especially to the problems of styles, that is to say of the virtues of human conviction and communion….' Dalí, encouraged by this scientific support, attributed to the paranoiac image a degree of 'concrete irrationality', which he denied to his old enemies automatism and the dream. 'Lacan's work perfectly gives an account of the objective and "communicable" hyperacuity of the phenomenon, thanks to which the delirium takes on this tangible character, which is impossible to contradict, and which places it at the very antipodes of the stereotypes of automatism and the dream. Far from constituting a passive element opening the way to interpretation…as those do, paranoiac delirium already constitutes in itself a form of interpretation.' With this concrete concept of irrationality, Dalí set out resolutely

The anamorphosis of the crane, a classic manneristic *memento mori*, is a theme in Dalí's work in the 1930s. In *Soft Skulls and Cranial Harp* (1935), above, the crane is either a part of or is being caressed by the monstrous hands of the 'average bureaucrat'.

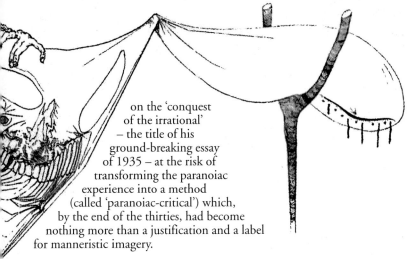

on the 'conquest of the irrational' – the title of his ground-breaking essay of 1935 – at the risk of transforming the paranoiac experience into a method (called 'paranoiac-critical') which, by the end of the thirties, had become nothing more than a justification and a label for manneristic imagery.

Flesh and form in revolt

The systematization of the confusion of reality becomes more refined. The dialectic between hard and soft, between mineral and organic, becomes more complex. The anamorphoses become the subject of the work. The unidentified object at the feet of Hans Holbein's *Ambassadors*, the secret and silent witness to man's inanity, comes to life. The anamorphic crane turns into a harp, allows itself to be milked by the 'average bureaucrat', and embraces the grand piano before viciously sodomizing it. Living beings themselves have difficulty holding onto their heads, whose tumescences are supported by crutches. Whole bodies are in revolt; the buttocks, elbows and knees of men are stretched and in their turn transformed into cranes. Bones stick out from beneath the dresses of women whose backs bulge with false, erectile breasts. Paralysed with frustration, muscles stiffen in the arc of the hysterical attack.

The borders between people and objects disappear. Powered by a secret mechanism, drawers spring from foreheads, stomachs and chests. Sheathed thighs from Vermeer serve as a table for a light meal. Conversely, objects come to life: tables have erections and participate in the passionate delirium of object cannibalism. This anthropophagic frenzy becomes suicidal. A monster with a ragingly ecstatic head tears itself apart in *Soft Construction with Boiled Beans* (1936), a picture that lent itself easily to being retitled *Premonition of Civil War*. Asked to illustrate *Les Chants de Maldoror*, Dalí combined the umbrella and the sewing machine with sacks of potatoes and the lecherous wheelbarrow of

Above: *Soft Construction with Boiled Beans* (1936), later called *Premonition of Civil War*, shows a monster destroying itself. Either heralding or recalling an apocalypse, the cannibalism of the 'object-beings' takes on a monumental force, made all the more powerful by the 'average bureaucrat'.

Millet's *Angelus*: Never could Lautréamont's antediluvian chaos have been better served than by the amorphous sado-masochism of his modern illustrator.

Above: *Burning Giraffe* (1936–37) accompanies two spectres with drawers.

In *The Invisible Man* (detail, left, and in full, below), dating from 1929–33, Dalí tackles the problem of abstraction in his own way. But the various architectural and figurative elements designed to conceal the main figure take on a strange reality of their own, like the Gala figures flattened against the steps. In the centre, beneath the obelisk formed by the perspectival shadows, is a 'modern-style ornamental object'

How to shock the Communists

André Breton applauded these provocations of delirium and supported Dalí against his own prudish Communist allies. *Le Surréalisme au Service de la Révolution* published an 'involuntary' *Rêverie*: a sequence of fetishist rituals designed to reproduce the emotions connected with a dream-like sodomization of Gala on

in the form of an anatomical basin containing an electric light bulb.

Right: *The Weaning of Furniture-Nutrition* (1934).

a dungheap in a stable. The debauching of an eleven-year-old girl by her mother – the narrator's lover – and by an old prostitute is staged in minute detail. We are spared none of the tumescences and detumescences that accompany the masturbation scene which ends with a fairytale metamorphosis in which the young girl is saved. Summoned to party headquarters, Louis

Aragon, Pierre Unik, Georges Sadoul and Maxime Alexandre – the only Surrealist members at the time – were preached to by a party functionary: 'All you're trying to do is complicate the simple, healthy relations between men and women.'

What Breton was not so happy about was Dalí's attempt to apply the conquest of irrationality to politics: 'Politics – there's something else that could currently become a "Surrealist speciality",' Dalí wrote to him in July 1933. 'In my view, we need to pay close attention to the Hitler phenomenon; I know officially that Georges Bataille is preparing a great panegyric to Hitler in the *Critique Sociale de Souvarine*, and that is something else that will somehow pass right under our "naz" [a play on the French word for "nose" and Nazi].'

Drunk with his media success in New York at the end of 1933, Dalí resumed the offensive, writing to Eluard: 'More and more seriously, I consider that Surrealism should evolve towards forming the basis of a new, anti-mystical religion, materialistic, founded upon the progress of scientific knowledge…a religion that would fill the imaginative, emotional void which the collapse of metaphysical ideas has produced in our time. I have very definite ideas on this subject, and I hope to talk to you personally about them, because I'm afraid that they might be interpreted differently.'

His fear was justified. On 23 January 1934, Breton sent him an ultimatum, accusing him of anti-humanitarianism, of wanting – through his emphasis

●I pressed myself closer and closer against the infinitely tender, unconsciously protective, back of the nurse, whose rhythmic breathing seemed to me to come from the sea…. I desired only one thing, which was that evening should fall as quickly as possible! At twilight and in the growing darkness I would no longer feel ashamed. I could then look Galuchka in the eye, and she would not see me blush. Each time I stole a furtive glance at Galuchka to assure myself with delight of the persistence of her presence…it seemed to me that [her glance], with the miracle of its expressive force, actually pierced through the nurse's back which from moment to moment was losing its corporeality, as though a veritable window were being hollowed out and cut into the flesh of her body.●

Dalí, *The Secret Life*

on the irrationality of the Adolf Hitler phenomenon – to dodge all revolutionary involvement, and finally of defending academic painting at the very moment when it was being extolled both by the Soviets and in Germany. In this context his latest painting, *The Enigma of William Tell* (1933), in which Dalí had provided a semi-nude Lenin with a gigantic, anamorphic buttock, was according to Breton a deliberate provocation, an academic piece that no longer deserved to be called Surrealist. Dalí replied two days later, repeating his point of view: 'No dialectical progress will be possible if one adopts the reprehensible attitude of rejecting and fighting against Hitlerism without trying to understand it as fully as possible.' But he voluntarily agreed to sign any declaration that did not contradict his previous writings. Nevertheless, on 2 February he could not resist exhibiting his gigantically buttocked Lenin at the Salon des Indépendants, where a band of Surrealists tried in vain to destroy it. It was all too much, and on the evening of 5 February he was summoned to the home of André Breton to face possible expulsion. Dalí transformed the 'trial' into a happening. Feigning a throat infection, he arrived with a thermometer in his mouth, wearing numerous sweaters which he proceeded to discard according to his temperature; he knelt before Breton, and explained to him that his attitude towards Lenin and Hitler had nothing to do with politics. 'Are you going to carry on boring us for much longer with your Hitler?' Breton intervened brusquely. And Dalí pleaded that he was not responsible for the obsessions that came out of his unconscious. 'It's like this, André Breton, I concluded, if tonight

According to Dalí, *The Enigma of William Tell* (1933), below, possibly described one of the most dangerous moments of his life. William Tell is Dalí's father, while the artist is the small child whom he holds in his arms and who, instead of an apple, has a raw cutlet on his head. According to Dalí, this is symbolic: it shows that William Tell has cannibalistic

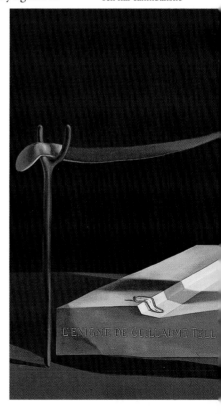

L'ENIGME DE GUILLAUME TELL

I dream that I am making love to you, tomorrow morning I shall paint our best sexual positions in the greatest detail.' Breton froze, his pipe clenched between his teeth, and mumbled furiously: 'I wouldn't advise you to do that, my friend.' Dalí had touched a nerve. It was not just a matter of knowing which of them would dominate the other, but also by linking Breton to homosexual exploits, Dalí had pinpointed the most dubious element of his character. While not turning a hair at the masturbation practised by a young girl in *Rêverie*, and boasting about sodomy with his companions, when it came to 'pederasty' it was said that Breton felt a kind of panic-stricken detestation. At a Surrealist meeting dedicated to sexuality, disregarding intentions and wants to eat him. Beside William Tell's foot there is a tiny walnut which contains a sort of cradle, and this cradle contains a tiny child who is the image of Gala. She is permanently under threat from the foot, which can crush the nut, the cradle, and can also destroy Gala if it moves just a fraction.

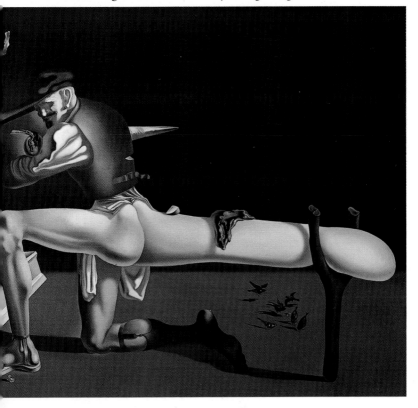

the loyal friendship avowed to him by René Crevel, he had accused 'the pederasts of proposing for human tolerance a mental and moral defect which tends to set itself up systematically and paralyse all the enterprises that I respect.' Dalí signed a declaration that he was not an enemy of the proletariat, and it was left at that. Up until 1938, Breton continued to show his affection for Dalí. Breton went on advocating the 'paranoiac-critical method', which at one stage he tried to replace with his concept of 'objective chance', before returning on the eve of the War to his beloved automatism.

Multiple images and morphological echoes

Itself an example of the paranoiac vision, the double image changes during the thirties into a multiple image:

According to Claire Pelissié, Dalí found the motif of the sleeping woman in *Invisible Sleeper, Horse, Lion* (1930), left, in a composition by Jules Romains in the Ducal Palace in Mantua. The bleeding pectorals of Patroclus, who is being supported by Achilles, are seen by Dalí as a woman's breasts, and the face and arm could in turn easily be taken for the nearby heads of the warhorses.

Invisible Sleeper, Horse, Lion (1930) presents itself *a priori* as chaos out of which there emerge under the attentive or even inattentive eye (such is the ambiguity of the paranoiac view) figures that have remained hidden until then. Out of the central deformity come the sleeper, the horse or the lion, all according to the lines and forms that take precedence, and this chance element of the picture throws up other figures that are recurrent in Dalí's work, such as the fellating couple multiplying over the surface of the canvas. Dalí describes as 'morphological echoes' this duplication of themes that

correspond to one another in various disguises, like 'the little girl skipping' and the 'bell in its belfry'. In *Suburbs of the Paranoiac-Critical Town: Afternoon on the Outskirts of European History* (1936), the skull, the bunch of grapes and the horse's hindquarters introduce a game of correspondences between obsessional elements that evoke Lacan's 'iterative identification of the object': 'fantasies of cyclical repetition, ubiquitous multiplication, endless periodic recurrence of the same events.' In 'The Conquest of the Irrational', Dalí affirms that the paranoiac-critical activity does not consider

In *The Dream* (1931), above, the woman with closed eyes and lustful mouth evokes certain Art Nouveau sculptures of women.

Surrealist phenomena and images in isolation but, on the contrary, in a coherent ensemble of systematic and significant relationships. The anthropomorphic landscapes are another means of illustrating the paranoiac vision but, unlike Giuseppe Arcimboldo (1527–93) or Josse de Momper (1564–1635), Dalí works not so much by addition as by dispersal of the elements that make up the face of, say, *The Great Paranoiac* (1936) or *Woman's Head in the Form of a Battle* (1936). The 'conversion of the real' works by inverting the basis and the form, and towards 1938 its painstaking techniques become increasingly complex (*Apparition of Face and Fruit Dish on a Beach*).

The shame that drives a man into hiding his face appears in Dalí's work around 1930. Is its origin paranoid? *The Great Paranoiac* (1936), above, suggests that it is, according to Ian Gibson: this is the most ambiguous version of the 'morphological echo' and the 'double image' where one can detect the influence of Leonardo and Arcimboldo.

The most famous of these optical puzzles, *The Endless Enigma* (1938), while allowing for six different images according to one's standpoint, leaves one somewhat sceptical as regards the 'delirious' coherence of the 'active and systematic structure'. The term 'conquest' is too tactical – it seems to imply that the irrational has been made to disappear. The systematization of confusion has now gone over the top: *Slave Market with Disappearing Bust of Voltaire* (1940) is little more than an optical game.

This doing-to-death of a technique corresponds to a change in Dalí's attitude towards the outside world. The iconoclastic celebration of a chaotic and morbid vision, as illustrated by the cannibal fantasies of 1934, is replaced in 1937 by a desire for form and Renaissance. A symbolic work, *The Metamorphosis of Narcissus* (1937), is accompanied by a poem and, like *The First Days of Spring* eight years earlier, it reveals a desire for renewal.

'Beneath the breach in the black cloud drifting away, the invisible scales of spring oscillate in the new April sky….' There follows a description of a vernal landslide that topples Narcissus down from the immaculate

From *The Great Paranoiac* to the *Slave Market with Disappearing Bust of Voltaire* (1940), below, one can see the refinement of a process which loses its power as it enhances its virtuosity. The labyrinthine ambiguity of the image gives way to an obligatory routine, even if the anatomical details and the distorted figures in the background still hold our attention. The gratuitousness of the portrait is reinforced by the accuracy with which the philosopher's face is reproduced, and it is made doubly incongruous by the Spanish setting.

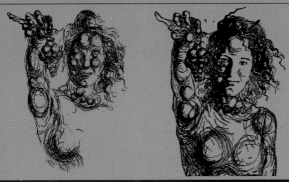

Left: *Suburbs of the Paranoiac-Critical Town* (1936), with its landscape format, presents a successive narrative in a similar way to medieval painting. The story begins on the right, in the Cadaqués street where Dalí's grandfather Gal lived; he was driven to suicide by his paranoia. This family secret weighed heavily on Dalí, who always considered Cadaqués (also the home of a girl-friend named Lydia) to be a veritable hive of paranoia. Gala welcomes us at the entrance to this town of interpretative delirium, holding out a delicious-looking bunch of grapes. Perhaps she is also offering us the key (clearly visible on the little cabinet, front right) that will allow Dalí to conquer the irrational. The bunch of grapes, as can be seen from the different preparatory sketches (above), has the same formal structure as the rear end of the horse, the skull and Gala herself. This sequence of morphological echoes leads us towards the left, to a temple suggested to Dalí by several buildings in Palamós when he painted this picture at the home of his friend José Maria Sert.

Double page overleaf: *The Metamorphosis of Narcissus* (1937).

mountain top to the shores of a lake, on which stand 'straight, tender and hard, the countless floral spears.' The youth with the 'clear and divine anatomy' loses himself, overwhelmed by his own reflection, when at the last moment he comes back to life in the morphological echo of 'the hand that bears the egg' from which emerges 'the flower, the new Narcissus, Gala, my narcissus.'

In *Suburbs of the Paranoiac-Critical Town*, Gala is holding a bunch of grapes in the middle of 'morphological echoes'. In *The Endless Enigma*, only by fixing his eyes on a single spot can the observer escape the 'endless' round of invisible images. The new Narcissus, Gala, at the same time mother and brother, expresses the chance for the young Dalí – through a duplicated narcissism – to escape from both the dread of homosexuality and the 'heterosexual' terror represented in the painting by the 'group' that bears this name. The positive concept of narcissism as a 'mirror phase', to use the expression coined by Lacan around the same time, enables the child to become aware both of the unity of his hitherto fragmented body, and of his relationship to the world.

Right: *The Endless Enigma* (1938) is the last of the enigmas. Dalí had reached a point of no return. The picture moves from a beach at Cape Creus with the rear view of a woman to a boat, a philosopher at rest, the face of a big, one-eyed cretin, a greyhound, a mandolin, a fruit dish with pears, and finally a mythological monster. This painting exhausts the technique of the multiple image, and the triumph of ambiguity sounds its last fanfare. Invention has turned into a game, and the reality decomposed by the painter's eye comes together again in the figure of Gala, whose shadowy form may be discerned leaving the scene. Her eyes, which are fixed on the observer, seem to draw him 'towards new adventures'. Shown at Julien Levy's exhibition in New York, the picture remained unsold, as if the paranoiac image which Dalí describes in the catalogue as a constant in art history (from cave paintings to Leonardo da Vinci and Arcimboldo) were now renouncing its revolutionary virulence. Within ten years, the reality of Gala took it definitively into confusional surreality.

THE ENDLESS ENIGMA

BEACH OF CAPE CREUS WITH SEATED
WOMAN MENDING SAIL SEEN FROM THE
BACK, AND BOAT.

RECLINING PHILOSOPHER.

FACE OF THE GREAT ONE-EYED MORON.

GREYHOUND.

MANDOLINE, FRUIT-DISH WITH PEARS,
TWO FIGS ON TABLE.

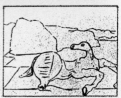

MYTHOLOGICAL BEAST.

Pampered by Breton and the Surrealists, the iconoclastic Dalí was also adored by high society. Launched by the 'Zodiac', a group of patrons, Dalí communicated his taste for provocative objects and Art Nouveau architecture, and he threw himself into the world of festivals, fashion and design.

CHAPTER 5

THE WORLD AND ITS DESIGNS: FROM OBJECT TO ARCHITECTURE

In *Portrait of Emilio Terry* (1930), left, Dalí has placed in the foreground a monster 'of symbolic functioning', which denigrates both the classical conventions of space and those of the sitter and architect, who was a Zodiac member.

An ironic photograph of Dalí, right, in the 'theatre of verdure' at the Villa Marlia, the home of Anna-Laetitia Pecci-Blunt.

Decorated by Jean-Michel Frank, the parchment salon of the Bischofsheim town house, left, brought together the classic collections and contemporary purchases of Charles and Marie-Laure de Noailles, seen below posing on the occasion of the 'Bal des Matières' ('Materials Ball') which they held in 1929.

Dalí's beginnings in Paris were easier than he makes out in *The Secret Life*. The financing of *L'Age d'Or* by Charles and Marie-Laure de Noailles put him in contact with the most elegant and fashionable couple in Paris. Even if Marie-Laure, a descendant of Laure de Sade, did not have quite the aristocratic background of her husband, she did own several areas of New York, thanks to the Bischofsheim inheritance, and was not short of a sou or two. Charles was not without means either, and they shared the ambition to take over from Etienne de

Beaumont, whose salon was a meeting-place for artists and high society and was immortalized in Raymond Radiguet's *Le Bal du Comte d'Orgel*. In their town house on the Place des Etats-Unis, they built a cinema in the old ballroom, with its Solimena ceiling, and there the 'happy few' enjoyed the privilege of watching *Un Chien Andalou* and *L'Age d'Or*.

At great expense, French designer Jean-Michel Frank (1895–1941) transformed the drawing room with white parchment and a mica fireplace, and here the couple exhibited their modern canvases alongside the masterpieces handed down by the family. Though Charles's taste was on the Classical side, he was fascinated by the Cubists, and by the 'Ingresque' Picasso, but Marie-Laure lured him into the mysteries of the Surrealists. In 1928 they acquired two Mirós, three Ernsts and two Tanguys. In 1929 they added three de Chiricos (of which two were bought from Eluard), one Ernst, and the original collages of Alberto Giacometti's (1901–66) *Woman with a Hundred Heads* and *Gazing Head* (bought from Jeanne Bucher). Dalí was invited to the Place des Etats-Unis in autumn 1929, and Charles – less of a prude than Breton – bought *The Lugubrious Game* for 7,000 francs, and *The Enigma of Desire* for more than double that price.

In 1930 he paid 10,000 francs each for *The Dream* and *Invisible Sleeper, Horse, Lion*, and the following year he gave Dalí 20,000 francs to buy a fisherman's shack in Port Lligat, in exchange for *The Old Age of William Tell*, which occupied the place of honour in the Frank drawing room. It was also Charles who acquired the emblematic *The Invisible Man* and who commissioned Dalí to do a *Portrait of Marie-Laure de Noailles* in 1933.

The Zodiac: an association of patrons

The Noailles were not the only ones to celebrate the new painter, whose social bearing had now changed from timidity to outright provocation. A group of patrons

Hung above the mica fireplace was *The Old Age of William Tell* (1931), below, which Dalí gave to the Noailles in exchange for a cheque. The money enabled him to buy a little house in Port Lligat, after he had been forced to leave his father's house. It was there, in the neighbouring olive grove, that Dalí, Gala and their friend René Crevel set up the scene with drapes and columns for their photography sessions

in the summer of 1931 (see p. 57). William Tell, the Swiss hero, was honoured by Dalí in the painting of the same name (p. 64), but here becomes a sinister image of the father threatening the growing love between Dalí and Gala, who are tied up on the left. On the right, they are seen fleeing the distressing scene.

gathered round him at the end of 1932 to guarantee him a fixed income, and every month there was a lottery enabling one of them to choose a work, with a final picture being added at the end of the year.

This collection of benefactors was indicative of the 'smart set' that launched Dalí. They were, in alphabetical order: Caresse Crosby, who with her husband Harry had founded the Black Sun Press and who introduced Dalí to the United States; Margaret (Tota) Cuevas de Vera, who was introduced to Dalí by Miró; the fashion photographer André Durst; the Prince de Faucigny-Lucinge and his wife Baba, née d'Erlanger; the writer Julien Green and his sister Anne, each of them members in their own right; the publisher René Laporte; Charles and Marie-Laure de Noailles; the Comtesse Anna-Laetitia (Mimi) Pecci-Blunt, hostess of the Villa Marlia; Felix Rolo, a friend of Christian Bérard's; Robert de Saint-Jean, a diplomat; and finally Emilio Terry, an architect.

'The day before yesterday I went to Dalí's to pick up my picture, as it is my month,' Julien Green wrote in his *Journal.* 'I can choose between a large painting whose background is an admirable landscape of rocks…and a small painting of marvellous hues, grey and lilac, plus two drawings. I'm choosing

A slim Dalí by the swimming pool at the Villa Marlia, together with Jean Rouvier and Anna-Laetitia Pecci-Blunt, a member of the Zodiac and hostess at the villa. She was a niece of Pope Leo XIII, and also a client of Jean-Michel Frank, who designed a salon in her Parisian town house with straw-covered walls. It was Frank who asked Dalí to design a sofa in the shape of Mae West's lips (below left) together with some screens.

Pecci-Blunt is to be seen overleaf on the left, together with the architect Emilio Terry (who worked with Frank) at the 'Marcel Proust Ball', in the home of Prince and Princess de Faucigny-Lucinge, members of the Zodiac. On the right: Emilio Terry and Jean Rouvier are to be seen flanking Princess 'Baba' de Faucigny-Lucinge at the 'Materials Ball' given by Charles and Marie-Laure de Noailles in 1929 at their town house on the Place des Etats-Unis. Among the guests were Paul Morand, Max Jacob, Louis Aragon, Max Ernst, Dalí and Gala. Included in the programme were Francis Poulenc's *Aubade* and a projection of 'gothic' images by Jean Hugo.

the small painting.' In the Zodiac, Emilio Terry's role was somewhat different from the rest. He was an amateur architect who collected treatises by the great masters – Andrea Palladio (1508–80), Claude-Nicolas Ledoux (1736–1806), Giovanni Battista Piranesi (1720–78) – and he also owned two delightfully anachronistic Neo-Classical houses. Along with Diego and Alberto Giacometti and Christian Bérard, he collaborated with the designer Jean-Michel Frank, and Dalí joined them with a design for some screens and a sofa in the form of Mae West's lips, attracting her victims like a carnivorous plant. The Baron de L'Espée, a client of Frank's, installed it at the centre of his 'cinema hall', beneath a bird by Giacometti.

Surrealist objects on a film set

Dalí had long since left behind what he saw as the sanitized world of nickel and paint, as represented by Le Corbusier. Since 1930, the 'attempt at the systematic confusion of reality' characterized by the paranoiac experience had entered the domains of architecture, objects and design.

Diametrically opposed to the immaculate functionality of 'cruise-liner' aesthetics, Dalí was the first – from 1929 onwards – to revive Art Nouveau architecture, which had fallen badly out of favour. It was Dalí who brought the works of Gaudí and Hector Guimard (1867–1942) back into fashion by getting Man Ray and Brassaï (1899–1984) to photograph them in 1933. Far from seeing them as possible sources for the twentieth century (as Nikolaus Pevsner and the Modernist theoreticians did), Dalí considered what he called the 'Modern Style' as a necessary and 'juicy' regression to the organic curves of the cave and the maternal womb. Under the influence of Otto Rank, the 'prodigal son' of Freud, rounded buttocks and vaginal slits decorate the 'intra-uterine' interiors of his designs, with the intention of making one forget the 'traumatism of birth'.

This 'Modern Style' architecture was the 'true realization of solidified desires where the cruellest, most violent automatism painfully betrays hatred of reality and the need for refuge in an ideal world, as is to be found in childhood neurosis,' Dalí wrote in 1933 in *Minotaure*. He refused to make this into a new aesthetic

Millet's *Angelus* was one of Dalí's obsessions: the figures of the two peasants bending towards the earth are interpreted as an 'expectant' preliminary to passionate, cannibalistic embraces. The man's hat fails to hide an erection which must be faced by the protagonists in this personal mythology. The couple are petrified in the *Architectonic Angelus of Millet* (1933), above, in biomorphic forms that precede the Manhattan buildings of 1934 with their erotic frenzy. Dalí's style veers towards Expressionism.

The peasant figures of the *Angelus* are to be seen on the horizon of the *Imperial Monument to the Child Woman* (*c.* 1930), left, along with other heroes of Dalí's mythology: the Mona Lisa, and Napoleon at the head of his army during the French campaign. Standing on the cypress shores of Arnold Böcklin's *Island of the Dead*, the 'paranoiac rock', inspired by petrified forms on Cape Creus, is nothing less than the erection of the 'solidified desires' (masturbation, bulging buttocks, erectile breasts) of a Dalí torn between fear (the son in disgrace, William Tell, the bird of prey, the androgynous jug, the lion masks) and the attractions of desire (the delicate bust of the child woman). The informal naturalism which Dalí had discovered in the Art Nouveau of Barcelona is conveyed in organic forms by the petrified waves or smoke. The Roman ruins place this Catalan Renaissance in the Mediterranean and Roman tradition of Ampuria. The tiny, exhausted figure of the Great Masturbator in the foreground is nothing more than a decorative object of gilded bronze on a lapis lazuli socle.

ideal, but saw 'ornamental architecture' as 'psychic decorativism' to catalyse all perversions.

Art Nouveau decoration, to be seen in *The First Days of Spring*, shows this regression into a polymorphous libido that is incarnated by multiple images (testicle-breasts, mouth-vaginas), such as abound in *The Lugubrious Game.* The tail of *The Great Masturbator* ends in Art Nouveau volutes which we see multiplied around the chalice in *Profanation of the Host*. The ambiguity of Art Nouveau curves and softnesses deprives them of any functional legitimacy, whereas paradoxically in the abstract such natural forms

L eft: *The City of Drawers* (1936).

B elow: *The Shoe* (1974).

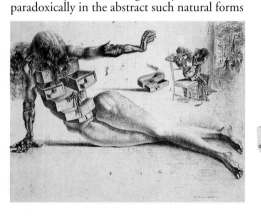

take on a Surrealism which the paranoiac eye can easily interpret.

In the *Imperial Monument to the Child Woman* (*c.* 1930), the scattered decorations melt into haunting metamorphoses: the foam from the wave, the smoke from the cigarette. Women's breasts become petrified while strange images emerge from the organic amorphousness of an oversize buttock or mouths welded with fear: eagle, lion, William Tell, woman-jug. The *Monument* is Dalí's three-dimensional version of Leonardo da Vinci's paranoiac wall. This 'realization of solidified desires', which from 1933 onwards evokes his

'houses for living madmen' or 'houses for erotomaniacs', is apparent in *The Architectonic Angelus of Millet* (1933) and *Atavistic Remains after the Rain* (1934). The architect Emilio Terry cautiously went along with Dalí, under whose influence his work became more curved and more dynamic, sometimes even covered with paranoiac drapes. But the 'snail house' that Terry exhibited in 1933 at the Jacques Bonjean Gallery, and in 1936 at the 'Fantastic Art, Dada, Surrealism' exhibition, Museum of Modern Art, New York, was a timid affair, as Dalí showed – not without a certain cruelty – in his 1934 portrait of his patron (p. 90). A mysterious cluster of lecherous, turgescent cranes disrupts the Classical space and seems to mock the architect's timidity.

Paranoiac confusion

In a 1933 article for *Minotaure*, entitled 'Concerning the Terrifying and Edible Beauty of Art Nouveau

Formerly part of Dalí dealer François Petit's collection, this *Cannibalism of Objects* (1932), above – more than a metre wide – is now one of the highlights of the drawings collection at the Musée National d'Art Moderne in Paris. A major classic of anamorphosis, the extended table has come to life, turning itself into a great sacrificial banquet at which objects and people tear each other apart, devouring one another in a desire for universal symbiosis.

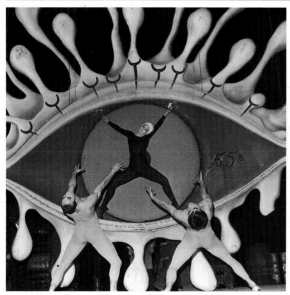

Architecture', Dalí corrected a formula that Breton had published in *Nadja*. He concludes: 'Beauty is none other than the sum total of the consciousness of our perversions. – Breton said: "Beauty will be convulsive or will cease to be." The new Surrealist age of "cannibalism of objects" equally justifies the following conclusion: Beauty will be edible or will cease to be.' (*The Collected Writings of Salvador Dalí*)

Paranoiac confusion takes over designs, furniture and even 'Surrealist objects', of which Dalí compiled a learned catalogue in *Le Surréalisme au Service de la Révolution*, where we see his first 'symbolically functioning object', based on the fetishism of the shoe and the unconscious effects of a piece of sugar dissolving in a glass of warm milk. Gala accompanied Dalí, to the great delight of René Crevel, who describes her irritating scourers scraping against bowls of flour in *Dalí, ou, l'Anti-Obscurantisme*, an enthusiastic appraisal of the artist's critical writings. André Breton and artist Valentine Hugo (1887–1968) were equally enthusiastic.

Surrealist exhibitions were also the setting for ephemeral happenings. In 1936, Dalí arrived at a

Following the initial sequence of *Un Chien Andalou*, the omnipresent eye became the prime phantasm from Dalí to Bataille of the 'Great Paranoiac's' erectile gaze. It dominated Maurice Béjart's 'Le Ballet du XXIe Siècle' ('Ballet of the Twenty-First Century'), above left, which was presented in 1962 at the Monnaie de Bruxelles and the Théâtre des Champs-Elysées.

The dream set in Alfred Hitchcock's *Spellbound*, with the many eyes of Cain vainly sliced by the castrating scissors of the hero, look down on the bare legs of the table where the plot begins to unfold. John Ballantine – the amnesiac double of the murdered doctor, played by Gregory Peck – describes his dream to Doctor Brulov. He says that he does not remember where he was, but he thinks that it must have been a gambling den. There were no walls, just curtains which were hanging down, with eyes painted on them. Ballantine then talks of a man who came in holding a large pair of scissors in his hand and started to walk round the room, cutting the curtains in half. Shortly after working with Hitchcock, Dalí worked with Disney.

London exhibition dressed as a deep-sea diver, in order to make his descent into the unconscious: the collector Edward James saved him at the last minute from asphyxiation. In 1938, at Georges Wildenstein's Galerie des Beaux-Arts, Dalí and Ernst as 'special advisers' organized a mannequin show in fantastic Parisian streets: Dalí's rainy taxi, with its female passenger covered with live Burgundy snails, was its most powerful image.

Living furniture

If objects come to life, furniture goes positively wild and undergoes daring metamorphoses of design: the 'lips' sofa is followed by the 'nose' fireplace, 'hair' curtains, and 'eye' frames – all forming the Surrealist apartment.

Fur seats with phantoms take root on the parquet floor of the drawing room, while divans with salivary glands attract unconscious odalisques. Elsewhere, rocking chairs designed as rib-cages invite one to relax in their depths. Hysterical cataleptics brace themselves, with breasts uplifted and drawers open. Not far away, an umbrella stand in the form of a phallus prepares to welcome detumescent umbrellas along the lines of the Lautréamont metaphor, while a standard lamp is made up of joined vertebrae.

The cinema, fashion and the stage

In a set designed for the Marx Brothers, wall lights in the form of hands cupped round a vagina with red pads close on the unsuspecting person who approaches them. For Alfred Hitchcock's *Spellbound*, Dalí designed a dream sequence in which a card table has a woman's legs, and an eye-covered piano wobbles off balance. Eroticized, animated, perverse, Dalí's furniture is full of 'Modern Style' volutes which reinforce its ambiguity.

Fashion also adopted the ideas of the artist, who befriended the two great rivals of the fashion world, Coco Chanel and Elsa Schiaparelli. The latter produced the 'hat with a cutlet' and the 'shoe hat'. She also designed a suit with drawer pockets which Cecil Beaton photographed for *Vogue* against settings inspired by Dalí's beaches. Again for *Vogue* André Durst photographed the collection of September 1939 against a background of mannequins with flaming heads who, according to the magazine, showed 'the influence of the painter S. Dalí on the domain of design'.

The stage was another medium through which Dalí was able to recycle various familiar icons, and give physical form to projects he had only sketched on paper. In autumn 1937, he signed a contract with Léonide Massine for the Monte Carlo Ballet, which included Christian Bérard, Eugène Berman and Étienne de Beaumont in the company. However, this *Mad Tristan* by Wagner and Nietzsche, the sketches for which were published by *Vogue* and included echoes of the *The Angelus of Millet*, did not see the light of day until two years later at the New York Metropolitan Opera, under the title of *Bacchanale* (1939). Coco Chanel, who had managed to oust Schiaparelli for the costumes, finally refused to supply them. In 1942 Dalí himself designed the sets and costumes for *Labyrinth* (1941), in which one of the sets depicted the gigantic torso of his 'average bureaucrat' against a Böcklin landscape.

Towards an architecture

Another patron, Edward James, took over in the mid-1930s. This Englishman, a writer and collector, made a dazzling entrance into Parisian high society when, following the advice of Marie-Laure de Noailles, he financed George Balanchine's *Ballet 33*, in which André Derain, Christian Bérard, Pavel Tchelitchew and Emilio Terry were all involved. Dalí met him in London in 1935; they came together again in Cadaqués

Along the lines of Giovanni Battista Bracelli's (1616–50) engravings, Dalí's *Venus with Drawers* (1964), far left, is the best-known example of the anthropomorphism of objects depicted by French draughtsman and engraver Jean Gérard Grandville in the nineteenth century. The powder puff tits and the belly drawer (empty) are not without what contemporary language called 'erotic allusions'. The autonomy of the 'little things', launched at the end of the 1920s, entered into the design of objects which, like architecture, took on a life of their own. In 1940 Dalí was the first to conceive sheep beds and sheep telephone stands. At an exhibition of Surrealist objects organized in 1936 by Charles Ratton, he displayed an 'aphrodisiac' smoking jacket. For Elsa Schiaparelli he dreamed up shoe hats which were worn by Gala and Baba de Faucigny-Lucinge. The motif of trompe-l'oeil tears in the textile of the dress pictured was used on the cover of the catalogue for the Dalí exhibition held at the Pompidou Centre in 1980.

during the summer, and in Italy during the autumn, and corresponded with each other. In November, James introduced Dalí to his architect, Hugh Casson, whom he had commissioned to renovate Monkton, his country house.

There was an immediate fusion of ideas: a violet coating, drainpipes in the form of palm trees, towels round the windows, four lip-sofas, padding and mirrors, not to mention the lobster telephone. The following year, on 10 May, James asked Dalí and Gala to send him some photographs of the rocks at Cape Creus, to decorate his drawing room in London. 'My architects tell me that the weight would be too great if I put pieces of real rock on the walls, and the house – which is old and fragile – would collapse under the strain. And so with some plaster, a bit of cement, and paint mixed with a few grains of mica, they are going to imitate this rock material…. But with the single little piece that I was able to show them, they didn't know how to create a large-scale view of those marvellous pitted formations.'

He gave Dalí a large advance to extend his house in Port Lligat, and, in June 1936, offered him a generous, exclusive contract which enabled James to acquire *Couple with Heads Full of Clouds* (1936), *Impressions of Africa* (1938), *The Great Paranoiac*, *Spain* (1938), *Sleep* and *The Creation of Monsters* (1937), and to build up one of the finest Dalí collections (now scattered).

Although Monkton, with its mixture of Regency furniture and Surrealist jokes, cannot be called a Surrealist interior, it was James who also financed what was to become Dalí's architectural masterpiece: the pavilion *Dream of Venus* at the 1939 World's Fair in New York. Back in 1934, during his first visit to the States, Dalí had already drawn Manhattan with all its hustle and bustle. Freeways allowed cars to race at will from one skyscraper to the next. Dalí even drew some

The photograph, above, was taken by Norman Parkinson. It shows the poet, collector and patron Edward James in his 'tent room' at 35 Wimpole Street, together with Igor Markevitch, sitting below Picasso's *Seated Woman with Hat* and Dalí's *White Calm* (1936). The bold sweep of the curtains recalls certain Surrealist decors by Terry and Pavel Tchelitchew's sets for the *Ballets 33* at the Théâtre des Champs-Elysées.

The lobster telephone, below left, the Mae West sofas, and the chair with upraised arms (an idea suggested by James), below, all helped to animate the Surrealist interiors of the various houses that Edward James wished to transform. In his London dining room he wanted to evoke the paranoiac rocks of Cape Creus, and elsewhere he dreamed of pulsating walls which Dalí wanted to cover with hair. James finally achieved his goal of creating a Surrealist environment after the war, at Xilitla in Mexico. His airborne pavilions and concrete fountains beneath tropical foliage are redolent of Dalí and Ernst, but also of the 'Jupiterian' houses of Victor Sardou, published by Breton in *Minotaure*, a review to which he subscribed.

of the buildings in the form of the peasant and peasant woman in *The Architectonic Angelus of Millet*.

In 1936 the exhibition 'Fantastic Art, Dada, Surrealism', organized by Alfred Barr at the Museum of Modern Art, contained a section devoted to architecture, including Gaudí and Guimard, Facteur Cheval whom Breton called an architect '*médiumnique*', Kurt Schwitters and his *Merzbau* (a kind of collage made from everyday detritus), and Emilio Terry and his *maison escargot* (snail house). In 1939, New York gallery owner Julien Levy entrusted Dalí with the project of a 'Surrealist pavilion' for the amusement area of the World's Fair. Dalí decided to call it *Dream of Venus* and, together with Gala and James, he set about assembling all the extravagances that had never found a patron. The façade of the pavilion, which borrowed some features from the coral grotto that Emilio Terry had designed in

1936 for the photographer Horst P. Horst, was both irregular and organic; rocaille competed with plaster drapes, and the entrance lay below the legs of a giant seated on a footstool. The irregular openings, spiked with pickaxes, corals or hands, offered glimpses of sculpted beauties such as the *Mona Lisa* and Sandro Botticelli's (1444/45–1510) *Venus* (she originally had the

head of a fish which the committee refused to sanction). Inside were two water tanks: 'One is filled with water and an incongruous assortment of objects, such as a plastic cow wrapped in bandages, like a mummy, a man made of rubber ping-pong bats, a fabulous deep-sea monster, a wobbling mass of plastic telephones, and a piano whose keyboard is painted on a rubber woman. In its choppy waters there are sirens with perfect bodies, splashing around in their flimsy costumes designed by Dalí.' The site was the scene of close teamwork: Gala, James, Julien Levy and many others joined in the task. The sirens' costumes were the subject of some dazzling photographs with which Horst P. Horst and George Platt-Lynes immortalized Dalí's ephemeral 'object-beings' decked out in their crustaceans and other *fruits de mer*.

Dalí (left, arriving in New York) was forced to give in to the petty-mindedness of his sponsors, who refused to let him endow his Venus with the head of a fish. This led him to issue a 'Declaration of Independence of the Imagination and the Rights of Man to His Own Madness'.

The *Dream of Venus* pavilion: The ticket office in the form of a fish lies beneath the raised skirts of a female giant.

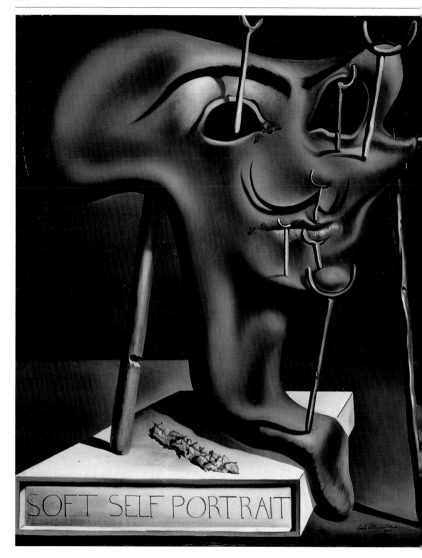

In 1942, while celebrating the marriage between psychoanalysis and morphology, Dalí announced that he had been converted to Classical form and Catholicism in *The Secret Life of Salvador Dalí*. The recycling of Surrealist imagery was duplicated by the painting of great 'mystical' canvases, under Gala's watchful eye.

CHAPTER 6

AVIDA DOLLARS RETURNS TO ORDER

Exhibited at the Julien Levy Gallery, this *Soft Self-Portrait with Grilled Bacon* (1941), left, announced the abandonment of psychological introspection in favour of a simple portrayal of the outer wrapping. Reduced to itself, the body with all its perverse distortions takes on a sublimated form – just as Man Ray's photo on the cover of *Time*, right, had done in 1936.

From psychology to morphology

The Metamorphosis of Narcissus proclaimed a metamorphosis in Dalí's work. The distortions and fragmentations suffered by the image since 1937 underwent one last paroxysm before giving way to the new cult of form. Parallel to this, the violence of the paranoiac vision, founded on the force of desire, veiled itself in religious reverence before *The Endless Enigma*. This work, which Dalí exhibited in 1939 at the Julien Levy Gallery in New York, gives full rein to the play of six images whose dizzy round ends in a formal void. In his preface to the catalogue, he trivialized his paranoiac intuitions by integrating them into a history of art ranging from the figures which the caveman drew on the rough stone of his dwelling, through the images by Arcimboldo and Bracelli, to the figures that inspired Piero di Cosimo. Too much paranoia kills paranoia, and this universal truth, announced from a 'Palladian' stage, heralded the fatal meeting between 'psychoanalysis, still in its infancy despite a brow lined with the delicate traces of sadness' and 'morphology, child of Goethe, a veritable angel'.

During his American exile, Dalí was made welcome by Caresse Crosby, a member of the Zodiac. He wrote *The Secret Life of Salvador Dalí*, and is seen below reading a passage from it in the drawing room at Hampton Manor in 1941. During Dalí's stay in New York, relations with other exiled Surrealists became strained: 'Yes, Dalí is a renegade,' declared Nicolas Calas in the June 1941 edition of *View*. The joint MOMA exhibition by Joan Miró and Dalí in November paradoxically widened the gulf.

Three years later, in the catalogue for a new exhibition at the Julien Levy Gallery, under the title 'The Last Scandal of Salvador Dalí', Dalí proclaimed Johann Wolfgang von Goethe's (1749–1832) victory over Freud. Retrospectively adapting his Surrealist attitude to the contemporary situation in Europe, he announced a second 'return to order' and a change from a 'psychological' period to a 'morphological' one: '…during these chaotic times of confusion, of rout and of growing demoralization, when the warmed up vermicelli of romanticism serves as daily food for the sordid dreams of all the gutter rats of art and literature, Dalí himself, I repeat, finds the unique

attitude towards his destiny: TO BECOME CLASSIC!' (*The Collected Writings of Salvador Dalí*) At the opposite extreme to the 'The Rotten Donkey' and Art Nouveau, there now appears the serene form, as characterized by the ideal architecture of the Escorial, of Donato Bramante (1443/44–1514) and Raphael. 'Finished – the epoch of improvised dramatic-lyrical blotches, of irresponsible spontaneous drawing, of two-cent philosophy disguising the technical and spiritual nothingness of the gratuitous, the shapeless and malformed. The young inquisitorial severity of the morphological era…already stands like a resplendent goddess at the temple gates of art, once more forbidding the unworthy to enter.'

How 'to become classic'

Judging by Dalí's work at the time, 'to become classic' was still nothing but a devout wish. Not only were his 'Palladian corridors' of 1938 peopled by manneristic

Above: *Daddy Longlegs of the Evening…Hope!* (1940) reveals the death throes of an imagery that has become bloodless. The forms vomited up by the cannon of world war struggle to rise again. The dialectic between hard and soft is reduced to a pulp, laid out in a geometrical structure that lacks conviction and is a staged iconographic compilation of contemporary elements.

spectres, but the soft became lifeless, as in *Daddy Longlegs of the Evening…Hope!* (1940), in which the Masturbator is merely a puddle. The work of the previous decade took an age to disappear, and the worn-out repertoire was taken up again, recycled in the lesser domains of book illustration, stage design, animated films, advertising, jewelry and society portraits. *The Geopolitical Child Observing the Birth of the New Man* (1943) says a lot about the improbable foetal rebirth that Dalí was simulating at the time in his photographic research with Philippe Halsman.

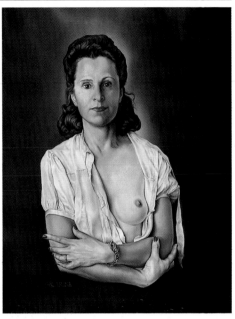

Only Gala, whose 1944–45 portrait *Galarina* sets out to achieve a certain Raphaelesque quality, fought against the triumphal downward spiral of Avida Dollars (Breton's anagrammatic nickname for Dalí). She alone personified his desire to become classic in the style of Bramante, as in *My Wife, Naked, Looking at Her Own Body, which is Transformed into Steps, Three Vertebrae of a Column, Sky and Architecture* (1945). And only through meeting her in the summer of 1929 had his life taken on a meaning, reviewed and corrected in the autobiographical mythology that constitutes *The Secret Life of Salvador Dalí*. From the 'intra-uterine memories' of the embryo to the dreams of the schoolboy, from the masturbations of the adolescent to the hallucinations of the adult, everything – the author tells us – heralded 'her who approaches', Gala or 'Gradiva', to echo the title of W. Jensen's novel *Gradiva*, which was immortalized by Freud and was very popular in Surrealist circles. In a year, thanks to Gala, Dalí's madness was apparently cured and his Surrealist demons vanquished. Dalí writes in *The Secret Life* that the conquest of the irrational,

Triumphant and lucid, the inspiration and muse has turned into the highly efficient Madame Dalí in *Galarina* (1944–45), above. Anaïs Nin recalled a stay at the Crosbys': 'And so each of us performed the task that had been given to us; Madame Dalí never raised her voice, she did not seek to seduce or to charm. Quite simply she judged that everyone was there to serve Dalí, the great and indisputable genius.'

This picture is entitled *My Wife, Naked, Looking at Her Own Body, which is Transformed into Steps, Three Vertebrae of a Column, Sky and Architecture* (1945). The dream of an architecture commensurate with human proportions was revived with the myths of the Renaissance. 'I can also say of Gala seated that she has the same grace as Bramante's Tempietto, near St Peter's Church in Montorio in Rome. And just like Stendhal in the Vatican, I too can measure the slender columns of her pride, the tender and stubborn balustrades of her childhood, and the divine stairways of her smile.' This anthropomorphic vision is the exact opposite of the fusion of flesh and stone in 'Concerning the Terrifying and Edible Beauty of Art Nouveau Architecture'. Having left a sanitized, architectonic world, under the aegis of Le Corbusier, Dalí only lingered in the anarchic world of Art Nouveau in order to restore all its potency to form. From then on, the hysterical sculptures that emerged from the organic convolutions of stone were domesticated within the framework of Classical architecture.

which he was set on, was already the essence of Catholicism. The irrational gave him certain secrets, he adds, which he guarded carefully while persevering in his destructive conquest and trying to carry with him the whole Surrealist group.

To read *The Secret Life* one would think that this 'need for order', mixed with a nostalgic desire to return to the bosom of the Catholic Church, had always been a part of Dalí, and that the Surrealist adventure was nothing but the sowing of wild oats along the path to notoriety. By representing himself as St John brandishing the cross before a Europe under threat from a drunken aeroplane, he announces in broad daylight the happy ending of his book. One thing is certain, he says: that nothing, absolutely nothing in the philosophical, aesthetic, morphological, biological or moral discoveries of our time is a negation of religion. On the contrary, according to Dalí the architecture of the temple of the individual sciences keeps its windows open towards heaven. Heaven is what he has been searching for all

A tomically levitated, Gala appears again in *Leda Atomica* (1949), below.

the time, he says, and through the density of a flesh corrupted and demonic, all his life.

A superstar Madonna

These tones of repentance, designed to please his new American friends and the new Spain of Franco must have gladdened the hearts of those exiled Surrealists who, like André Breton, had retained some affection for him. The 'Conquest of the Irrational', which Dalí began in 1935, finished quite simply with its elimination. Dalí found himself face to face with naked reality the name of which, from now on, as he emphasizes once more in the last lines of *The Secret Life*, was Gala.

But the triumphant and fierce Gala of *Galarina* was to change after the War into a wax doll. Astonishingly rejuvenated, and looking as unnatural as the stuffed swan which she is embracing, *Leda Atomica*, like *Madonna of Port Lligat*, belongs to the culture of posters and picture postcards. She is one of the 1950s canvases in which the artist tried, like a nuclear-age Leonardo da Vinci, to combine science and mysticism, and to inspire religious fervour by bringing to life the apocalyptic spectre born on Bikini Atoll. We find her again in *Assumpta Corpuscularia Lapislazulina* (1952), or as a Madonna gazing at a blond Christ, a superstar Madonna before her time, in *Corpus Hypercubicus* (1954) or in *Santiago El Grande* (1957). And she crops up again as St Helena, draped in a pennant, in *The Dream of Christopher Columbus* (1958–59), and under the burnous of a knight in *The Battle of Tetuan* (1960).

Gala and Dalí had good reason to celebrate the discovery of a continent that brought them fame and fortune. Commissioned by Huntington Hartford, one of the biggest grocers in America, for his Columbus Circus Gallery, *The Dream of Christopher Columbus* (1958–59), below, was one of Dalí's large-scale

compositions (410 x 284 cm) at which his aide, Isidor Bea – a specialist in opera sets – excelled. Bea's virtuosity with clouds saved Dalí a great deal of precious time. Dalí, who thought that like all geniuses Columbus was a Catalan, regarded this victory by the predecessor of Avida Dollars as a triumph for Christ and the Virgin as incarnated by Gala – levitating as usual, with the folds of her robe decorously covering the nudity of the young Adonis leading the way of the cross and the halberd.

A mystical manifesto

Atomic disintegration had little effect on the 'new morphological era'. Nero's nose, the pips of the pomegranate or the watermelon, the inkwell and the swan's head, Mantegna's egg, the architectonic elements of Leda's throne, the Madonnas – all evince a detachment that is inscribed in the lines of an eternal harmony. Above a world that was torn by impotence and anarchy Dalí, in his 'Mystical Manifesto' of the night of 15 April 1951, glimpsed the radiant future of a 'mystical painting' inspired by the theory of relativity and by an absolute monarchy: 'Absolute monarchy, perfect aesthetic dome of the soul, homogeneity, unity; biologocal, hereditary, and supreme continuity – all this above, brought up near the dome of the sky. Below, swarming and supergelatinous anarchy, viscous heterogeneity, ornamental diversity of ignominious soft structures compressed and yielding the last juice of their ultimate forms of reactions. "Anarchic monarchy," this is the "(almost divine) harmony of opposites" proclaimed by Heraclitus, which only the incorruptible mold of ecstasy will knead one

This *Christ of St John of the Cross* (1951), above, inspired by a drawing attributed to the mystic of Avila, hovers above Port Lligat.

day with new stones from the Escorial.' (*The Collected Writings of Salvador Dalí*) Or: how to reconcile the classes in Franco's Spain while waiting for a restoration.

With the minute brushwork of a miniaturist, the 'great machines' in which Dalí mixed the old Surrealist tricks with his latest optical inventions could never have taken on their extravagant dimensions had it not been for the help of Isidor Bea, a theatre and opera designer whom Dalí had met in 1955 and whose technological skills allowed these painstaking adaptations to be done on a large scale. Perhaps one can see in these illusionist processes – particularly in *Santiago El Grande* – a taste acquired when Dalí was designing sets for ballet and opera.

Apart from these religious images, the most successful of which is a *Christ* inspired by a sketch attributed to St John of the Cross, there were fortunately still a few monomaniac obsessions to stir the sleepy waters round the otherwise desperately becalmed shores where Dalí, 'at the age of six, when [he thought] he was a little girl, very cautiously [lifted] the skin of the sea to observe a dog sleeping in the shadow of the water.' Among these, as mystic as it is phallic, is the picture of a rhinoceros horn, born out of Dalí's attempts at the 'corpuscular' decomposition of anatomies, such as the *Exploding Raphaelesque Head* of 1951. Revered in China since ancient times for its aphrodisiac qualities, and copiously displayed in Renaissance cabinets of curiosities, this logarithmically curved appendage appealed to Dalí's penchant for the golden section. Like a new Luca Pacioli (*c.* 1445–1514), in quest of divine proportions, he discovered the curved horn in cauliflowers and in the pistils of

sunflowers, in Vermeer's *Lacemaker*, in the *baretta* of Catalan peasants, and even in the folds of the 'rhinocerotic' anus. In short, the horn was everywhere, to the great pleasure of the students at the Sorbonne. In 1955, Dalí announced to them: 'As for me, after this

Suspended in space, *Madonna of Port Lligat* (1949) has the same architectural solidity of her throne. The inversion of shell and egg, borrowed from Piero della Francesca's (*c.* 1415–92) *Madone*, confirms the negation of natural laws. The gateway opening through the bodies of the mother and child fulfils the idea of the icon as a gateway open to heaven. The metaphor is echoed by the sea urchin, whose spiral structure opens out like the cupola of the Roman Pantheon onto the divine azure. The light that separates the sea from the architectonic hills of Port Lligat accentuates still further the impression of levitation.

evening's talk, in truth I think that to have moved from the *Lacemaker* to the sunflower, from the sunflower to the rhinoceros, and from the rhinoceros to the cauliflower, one must really be or have a bee in the bonnet.'

Science and religion

Other fantasies more connected with his flesh and his biography bring us back to the fragmented anatomies of 1929, with the dislocated world of sacred objectivity. We are faced again with death and blood, two mysteries that the clear, clean surfaces of the morphological period cannot mask.

This is to be seen for instance in *Tunny Fishing* (1966–67), where the captured fish are finished off between the boats with savage harpooning that reddens the foaming waters of the sea. These shining bodies in a confined

Above: *Rhinocerotic Disintegration of Illisus of Phidias* (1954).

Below: Dalí by Philippe Halsman.

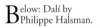

space are meant to illustrate the ideas of one of the great philosopher-theologians of the age, the Jesuit Teilhard de Chardin, who like Dalí buckled under the immense task of reconciling science and religion, from prehistory to the nuclear age. *Tunny Fishing* shows that the Old master was still able to extract turmoil from the callipygous curves and the Michelangelo necks of the fishermen and the 'tunaesque' thighs of the Pergamene Tritons – all airbrushed to perfection. With his eyes finally open, the old Masturbator created in this gigantic orgy a convincing homosexual icon.

The *Hallucinogenic Toreador* continues and rounds off these adventures by way of images, with their deaths and resurrections, in a last foreshortening which compresses into a single constellation – under the gaze of the child Dalí – the life of forms. This immense picture, which is divided into twelve parts, is a retrospective rebus depicting the painter's various obsessions, all dominated by the Venus de Milo whose torso, reproduced on a box of pencils had revealed the face of a toreador to Dalí. This 'double image ready-made' – to use Ian Gibson's expression – recalled the death of the toreador in Lorca's *Lamentation*: 'Oh white wall of Spain, oh black bull of anguish', as well as the death of Lorca himself, who died like a hero at the hands of his own people. There is no doubt that the memory of Lorca and his 'Ode' would have been accompanied by feelings of regret when Dalí returned to order and to Spain.

Gris's Cubist chair, the 'nuclear particles' surrounding the head of the bull, the peasant woman from the *Angelus* in the shadow of Venus, the flies of Gerona buzzing round a 'Chien Andalou visiting Perona Cave' at Cape Creus – this whole picture, Dalí told author Luis Romero, represented lost friends, from his elder brother, Pierre Batcheff (who acted in *Un Chien Andalou*), René Crevel, right through to Lorca, who is alluded to by the toreador's green cravat. The de Chirico arches of the arena and the guardian angels at the central gate suggest both the moon and the nocturnal ascent of

D alí remained true to himself by playing off form against disintegration, but the dark and melancholy ambiguity of the head of *The Great Paranoiac* (p. 82) gave way in *Exploding Raphaelesque Head* (1951), below, to the brilliance of a sunbeam penetrating the fontanelle of Hadrian's Pantheon. The anthropomorphism of architecture, theorized by Vitruvius, is apparent here, with

the cupola opening up to the sky as part of Dalí's new Roman Catholicism. Proof of the existence of God comes via dematerialization, which reveals the 'spirituality of all substance', as Dalí affirmed in the 'Mystical Manifesto' published at the same time.

Paul Ricard came to collect *Tunny Fishing* (1966–67), which measures 3 x 4 metres, from the Port Lligat studio in his yacht. By endowing this fishing scene with a sacrificial, erotic tone, Dalí was creating the nautical equivalent of Mithraic sacrifices; the blood boiling in the water becomes a pagan sign of regeneration, in which memories of Pergamum and of the Sistine Chapel mix with the pop icons of the advertising world.

the toreador's soul, mourned by Lorca in his poem. Medusan and spectral, the head of Gala has its eyes closed, present at and yet absent from this round of memories.

The final years were darkened by the death of Gala and by illness, and left little room for work from a trembling hand that needed too much guidance to be itself. The last photographs of the master, dressed for the occasion like a living god, scarcely flatter the artist, who was yielding to the pressures of his entourage with regard to the future of his rights, was signing white lithographs, was authorizing reproductions and fantasy editions that included some final objects – parodic interpretations of the bizarre – which only succeeded in devaluing Dalí's work for decades to come.

Avida Dollars or crossing the desert

Long before his death in 1989, Dalí had entered a kind of purgatory from which he found it difficult to emerge. The exhibition at the Georges-Pompidou Centre in 1980 had been a last-ditch stand. On the one hand, the orthodox Bretonians and Surrealist specialists ignored his work prior to 1929, and reduced the works of the thirties to a few 'optical games' and provocations, confining the paranoiac experience to the so-called 'paranoiac-critical method' – a formula that Dalí himself did not use until 1936, at the moment when he began his return to order. On the other hand, the Dalí supporters – the gullible and the enlightened – accepted without demur the revelations of *The Secret Life* and *Diary of a Genius*, as well as all the interviews granted by the master between the fifties and seventies, the clear aim of which was to muddy the waters and 'cretinize' the reader, to use an expression that Dalí borrowed from Lautréamont.

Close friends set themselves up as historians, dubious intermediaries passed judgment as to what was true and what was false, the universities were scornful, and the works disappeared behind the undisputed talent of the artist-magician that he had always been. However, since the research done by critics like Rafael Santos Torroella, and historians like Felix Fanes, Peter Gorsen and Haim Finkelstein, and after exhibitions such as 'Early Years'

While looking 'vaguely' at a box of Venus pencils, which was decorated with a Venus de Milo, Dalí thought he could discern the face of a toreador. In the painting, at the centre of the arena the morphological echo of Venus torsos is imperceptibly transformed into her back. *Hallucinogenic Toreador* (1969–70), right, is composed of twelve pictures, consisting of personal references watched over by the figure of a child in a sailor suit. Is Dalí trotting out the same old images? Luis Romero, who has devoted a whole work to this one painting, assures us that 'in order to make the best of images that are perhaps a little banal, but are also illuminating, we would say that Dalí neither plagiarizes nor imitates himself, but that he uses the materials taken from his own psychic and pictorial world which form part of his personal cosmogony. One might compare them to Balzac, whose characters appear in several novels and give a consistency and unity to the collected works. Dalí's oeuvre is a sort of painted *Comédie Humaine* in which are mingled subconscious imagination and furious actuality.'

at the Tate Gallery in 1994 and those organized by the Gala Salvador Dalí Foundation, the paintings have undergone a revaluation, and the works have been viewed again from a critical perspective; thematic analysis has now learned to avoid both the key of psychoanalytical dreams and reliance on the retrospective confessions of the painter himself.

The first monograph worthy of the name is that by Ian Gibson, which at last puts all the legends into perspective. It brings to the fore three key characters in the artist's life: his father, Lorca and Gala – a vital constellation, of which countless archives and scattered private collections of correspondence will one day allow us to gain a better understanding.

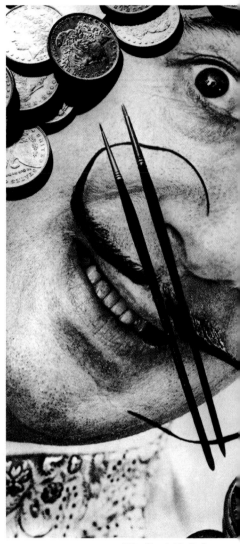

Dalí as Avida Dollars, by Philippe Halsman.

Above: *Perpignan Station* (1965) was painted shortly after the publication of the *Tragic Myth of Millet's Angelus*, a 'paranoiac-critical' interpretation which brought back to Dalí the iconography of the 1930s: Gala watches Dalí floating over his work. Higher up we can see the two oppressive figures of Millet's *Angelus* in a state of atavistic hibernation against a sky that is suddenly transformed into a gigantic Maltese cross in the middle of Perpignan Station, a nodal point at which all parts of the universe converge.

Overleaf: *Young Virgin Auto-Sodomized by her Own Chastity* (1954).

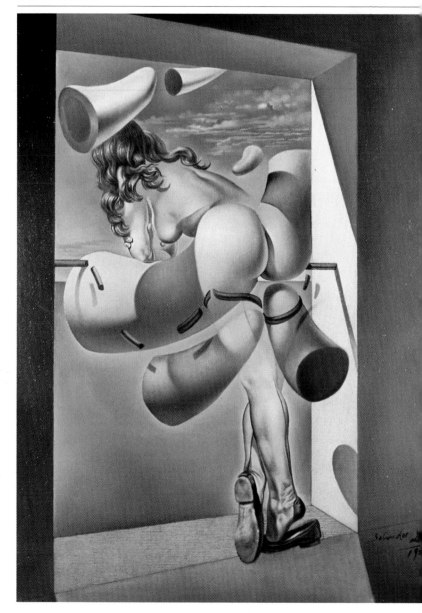

DOCUMENTS

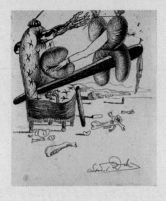

Dalí the writer

*The constant stream of provocative words from the
post-war Dalí made many forget his earlier theoretical
writings as a student and young painter. Critical views
on contemporary painting, photography and cinema
were accompanied by reflections on his own work, on the
phenomenon of vision, and on control of the unconscious.
These texts are crucial to our understanding of his
embrace of Surrealism.*

THEORETICAL WRITINGS

St Sebastian

…I realized that I was in Italy because
of the black-and-white patterning of the
marble staircase. I climbed up it. At the
top was St Sebastian tied to the trunk of
an old cherry tree. His feet were resting
on a broken capital. The more I looked
at his face, the more curious it seemed
to me. Having said that, I felt that I'd
known it for ever, and the aseptic light
of the morning revealed the tiniest details
with such clarity, such purity, that there
was no way I could be mistaken.

The saint's head was in two parts:
one was made of a substance similar
to a jellyfish, supported by a very fine
ring of nickel, the other a half-face that
reminded me of someone very familiar;
out of the ring came a very white
plaster-of-Paris support, which was
shaped into the spinal column of
the figure. All the arrows had their
temperature on them, and a little
inscription engraved in the steel read
'Invitation to the Coagulation of the
Blood'. On some parts of the body,

veins showed on the surface of the skin,
with the intense blue of a Patenier
storm, delineating the curves of a
painful voluptuousness on the coral-
pink of the skin….

From *L'Amic de les Arts*, 31 July 1927

The Rotten Donkey

An activity with a moral tendency could
be sparked off by the violently paranoiac
desire to systematize confusion.

The very fact of paranoia, and
especially consideration of its
mechanism as a force and a power, leads
us to the possibilities of a mental crisis
whose nature could be the equivalent to,
but at any rate is the direct opposite of,
the crisis to which we are also subjected
by the fact of hallucination.

I think the moment is near when,
through a process of thought that is
paranoiac and active in nature, it
will be possible (simultaneously with
automatism and other passive states)
to systematize confusion and to
contribute to the total discredit of
the world of reality….

As far away as possible from the
influence of the sensory phenomena

to which hallucination can consider itself to be more or less bound,paranoiac activity always uses controllable and recognizable materials. It is already enough that the delirium of interpretation has succeeded in linking the meaning of images in heterogeneous pictures covering a wall for no one to be able to deny the real existence of that link. Paranoia makes use of the external world in order to validate the obsessive idea, with the special, disturbing feature that it validates the reality of this idea for others. The reality of the external world serves as an illustration and a proof, and is put at the disposal of the reality of our minds.

All doctors agree in recognizing the speed and the inconceivable subtlety frequently to be found in the paranoiac who, armed with facts and themes so refined that they escape the grasp of normal people, reaches conclusions that are often impossible to contradict or reject and which, in any case, almost always defy psychological analysis.

It is through a clearly paranoiac process that it has been possible to create a double image: that is to say, the representation of an object which, without the slightest figurative or anatomical modification, is at the same time the representation of another absolutely different object, itself stripped of any kind of distortion or abnormality that might indicate that there has been some kind of arrangement....

From *La Femme Visible*, Paris, 1930.
Text dedicated to Gala Eluard.

'Paranoiac-critical interpretation of the obsessive image, Millet's *Angelus*'

...Consideration of the paranoiac mechanism as a force and power operating at the very basis of the phenomenon of the personality, of its 'homogeneous', 'total' character, and its features of 'permanence', 'growth', 'productivity', inherent in the systematic fact, can only be confirmed in the most rigorous manner by reading Jacques Lacan's admirable thesis, *On Paranoid Psychosis and its Relation to the Personality*. It is through this work that we can for the first time gain a homogeneous and comprehensive idea of the phenomenon, away from the mechanistic miseries in which current psychiatry is now bogged down. Its author is particularly opposed to the general ideas of constitutionalist theories, according to which systematization develops after the event, as a result of the workings of very vague constitutional factors that lead to the creation of such crude equivocations as 'reasoning madness'. The unilateral statism of this latter notion, by nullifying the concrete, genuinely phenomenological essence of the problem, drives away all the dazzling dialectical significance of the paranoiac process, which at this time cannot fail to strike us as absolutely exemplary. Lacan's work does full justice to the objective and 'communicable' hyperacuity of the phenomenon, through which delirium takes on the tangible and indisputable nature that places it at the opposite extreme to the stereotypes of automatism and the dream. Far from being a passive element inviting interpretation and open to intervention as those are, paranoiac delirium already constitutes a form of interpretation in itself. It is precisely this active element, born of the 'systematic presence' which, beyond the scope of preceding general considerations, intervenes as the principle behind this contradiction, which for me encompasses the poetic drama of Surrealism. There is no better way of dialectically resolving this contradiction than through the new ideas that shed light on paranoia, and according to which delirium emerges wholly systematized....

From the prologue to 'Nouvelles considérations générales sur le mécanisme du phénomène paranoïaque du point de vue surréaliste', in *Minotaure*, no. 1, 1933

Millet's *Angelus*, as beautiful as the 'chance meeting of a sewing machine and an umbrella on a dissecting table'

...There is no image that seems to me capable of a more literal, more delirious illustration of Lautréamont and, in particular, *Les Chants de Maldoror* than that which was created about seventy years ago by the painter of tragic, cannibalistic atavisms, of ancestral and horrific meetings between sweet, soft, good quality meats: I am alluding to Jean-François Millet, that painter who has been immeasurably misunderstood. It is precisely Millet's thousandfold famous *Angelus* which, according to me, is painting's equivalent to the well-known and sublime 'chance meeting of a sewing machine and an umbrella on a dissecting table'. In fact nothing seems to me capable of illustrating this meeting as literally and as atrociously and as hyperevidently as the obsessive image of *The Angelus*. *The Angelus* is, to my knowledge, the only picture in the world that depicts the stationary presence and the expectant meeting of two beings in a solitary, crepuscular and mortal environment. In the picture, this solitary, crepuscular and mortal environment plays the role of the dissecting table in the poetic text, for not only is life fading away on the horizon, but the fork is also plunging into this real and substantial flesh which

has always been the earth that man ploughs; it plunges in, I say, with the greedy, fertile intentionality characteristic of the delectable incisions of the bistoury which, as everyone knows, does nothing but secretly search in the dissection of every corpse, under various analytical pretexts, for the synthetic, fertile and nourishing potato of death; from which comes this constant dualism, sensed across all eras, of the ploughed earth – food, dining table, ploughed earth feeding itself on this shit sweet as honey which is nothing other than that of authentic, ammonia-filled, necrophiliac desires – a dualism that leads us finally to consider the ploughed earth, especially if it is deteriorating in the dusk, as the best served dissecting table, that which of all tables offers us the best guaranteed and most appetizing corpse, seasoned with that fine and imponderable truffle that can only be found in nutritious dreams made up of the meat of shoulders softened by Hitlerite, atavistic nannies, and with the incorruptible and exciting salt created by the frenetic and voracious swarming of ants, which should be part of any authentic 'unburied putrefaction' that respects itself and can pass as worthy of that name....

Extract from the catalogue preface to the Dalí exhibition at Quatre-Chemins, Paris, 1934

'The waters in which we swim'

...It is in these circumstances that Salvador Dalí, with the exact apparatus of paranoiac-critical activity in his hand and less prepared than ever to desert his intransigent cultural post, has long proposed that one should try to eat the Surrealists too, because we the Surrealists are the sort of food – good quality, decadent, stimulating, extravagant and ambivalent – which with a maximum of tact and in the most intelligent manner in the world fits in with the gamey, paradoxical and succulently truculent state that is right for and characteristic of the climate of ideological and moral confusion in which we have the honour and pleasure to live at this time.

For we the Surrealists, as you will be able to convince yourselves by observing us with a small amount of attention, are not exactly artists, and nor are we exactly men of science; we are caviar, and caviar – believe me – is extravagance and intelligence even of taste, especially at those concrete moments like the present moments when the irrational famine of which I am speaking to you, although immeasurable, impatient and imperialist, finds itself so exasperated by the salivary expectations of the wait that to begin with it needs – in order to achieve its next glorious conquests – to swallow the fine, intoxicating and dialectic grape of the caviar, without which the thick and stifling food of similar ideologies would threaten to paralyse from the start the vital and philosophical rage of the historical belly.

For if caviar is the vital experience of the sturgeon, it is also that of the Surrealists, because like the former we are carnivorous fish that, as I have already hinted, swim between two waters – the cold water of art and the warm water of science – and it is precisely in this temperature and swimming against the current that the experience of our life and of our fertilization achieves that confused profundity, that irrational and moral hyperlucidity that can only be produced in a climate of Neroesque osmosis created by the living and continuous fusion of the thickness of the sole and of crowned tepidity, of the satisfaction and the circumcision of sole and bowl, of territorial ambivalence and agricultural patience, of acute collectivism and visors held up by letters of white on the bands of the old villager and letters of white on the bands of the old pillager, of all those kinds of tepid and dermatological elements which in sum are the coexisting and characteristic elements that prevail in the notion of the 'imponderable', a mock notion unanimously recognized just in order to serve as an epithet for the ungraspable taste of caviar, and also a mock notion that already conceals the timid taste buds of concrete irrationality which, being nothing but the apotheosis and the paroxysm of this objective imponderable and consisting of the exactitude and the divisive precision of the actual caviar of imagination, will in an exclusivist and – over and above this – philosophical manner bring about the appallingly demoralizing and appallingly complicated result of my experiences and inventions on the pictorial level.

For one thing is certain: in all its forms, I hate simplicity.

From *La Conquête de l'Irrationnel*,
Paris, 1935

POETRY AND PROSE

'My girlfriend and the beach'

At this very moment, on the beach,
the printed letters of the newspaper are
in the act of eating the drowsy donkey,
rotten and clear-cut as mica.

We will all go to the place where
the slaughtered and pitiful beasts perish
with their little vein that has burst in
their flight which creaks and sweats
out little drops of serum. There we
shall break the plaster of the snails,
until we discover those which are within
and have tiny apparatuses of nickel,
sweet as honey and slightly feverish
because of the limpidity of their own
articulated perfections.

Now that I am perspiring under
my arms, I shall let die in its sponge
the subtle air emitted by all the
apparatuses of the beach, releasing
the joys of flying breasts, red and warm,
that drip with blood.

My girlfriend is stretched out with
her extremities tenderly divided up,
full of flies and little aluminium blades,
which race towards her naked, semi-
vegetable body that is coated with all
the mascara I gave her on her birthday.
My girlfriend has adorable ears. My
girlfriend has a body full of little holes
and as transparent as dry leaves
perforated with a brush and seen
against backlighting.

One morning I painted a newborn
babe which I then left to dry on the
tennis court. After two hours I found it
all bristling with ants that made it move
to the anaesthetized and silent rhythm
of sea urchins. Nevertheless, I realized
immediately that this newborn child
was none other than the pink breast
of my girlfriend, being frantically eaten
by the metallic and shining thickness
of gramophone needles. But it wasn't
her breast either: it was little pieces of
my cigarette paper nervously assembled
round the magnetized topaz of my
fiancée's ring….

From *L'Amic de les Arts*,
30 November 1927

The Great Masturbator

Despite the prevailing darkness
the evening was not yet far advanced
to the sides of the great stairways
of agate
where
weary of the light of day
that had lasted since the sunrise
the Great Masturbator
his huge nose leaning on the onyx
  parquet
his enormous eyelids closed
his forehead eaten away by terrible
  wrinkles
and his neck swollen by the celebrated
  boil
where the ants bustle
comes to a halt
preserved in this evening hour that
  is still too light
while the membrane that completely
  covers his mouth
hardens along the frightening and huge
  grasshopper
motionlessly clinging and sticking to it
for five days and five nights.
All the love
and all the intoxication
of the Great Masturbator
resided
in the cruel ornaments of fake gold
that covered his soft and delicate temples
imitating
the form of an imperial crown
whose fine leaves of bronzed acanthus
extend
as far as the pink and beardless cheeks
and continue their hard fibres

until they melt
in the clear alabaster of his nape.
        From *La Femme Visible*, Paris, 1930

The Metamorphosis of Narcissus

Narcissus is shattered in the cosmic
    vertigo
at the deepest depths of which
sings
the cold and Dionysiac siren of his
    own image.
The body of Narcissus empties itself
    and loses itself
in the abyss of his reflection,
like the hourglass that will not be
    overturned.
Narcissus, you are losing your body,
    carried away and confounded by the
age-old reflection of your disappearance,
your body struck with death
descends towards the abyss of topaz
to the yellow wrecks of love,
your body, white, engulfed,
follows the slope of the wildly
    mineral flood
of black stones with acrid scents,
your body…
as far as the matt mouths of the night
at the edge of which
already sparkles
all the red silverware
of dawns with burst veins in
'the jetties of blood'.
Narcissus,
do you understand?
Symmetry, divine hypnosis of
the geometry of the mind, already fills
    your head
with this slumber incurable, vegetable,
atavistic and slow
that dries up the brain
in the parchmented substance
at the heart of your imminent
    metamorphosis.
The seed of your head has just fallen
    into the water.

Man returns to the vegetable
through the heavy sleep of fatigue
and the gods
through the transparent hypnosis
    of their passions.
Narcissus, you are so immobile
one would think you are asleep.
If it were Hercules rugged and brown
one would say: he sleeps like a log
in the pose
of a Herculean oak.
But you, Narcissus,
shaped by timid blooms perfumed
with translucent adolescence,
you sleep like a flower of water.
Here comes the great mystery,
the great metamorphosis is about
    to happen.
Narcissus, in his immobility, absorbed
in his reflection with the digestive
    slowness
of carnivorous plants, becomes invisible.
Nothing remains of him
except the hallucinating oval whiteness
    of his head,
his head again more tender,
his head the chrysalis of biological
    ulterior motives,
his head held up by fingertips of water,
fingertips
of the crazy hand,
of the terrible hand,
of the coprophagic hand,
of the mortal hand
of his own reflection.
When this head will crack,
when this head will split,
when this head will explode,
it will be the flower,
the new Narcissus,
Gala –
my narcissus.
        From *Métamorphose de Narcisse*,
                Paris, 1937

The Surrealists' view of Dalí

When he arrived in Paris in 1929, Dalí was taken under the wing of André Breton, who wanted to snatch him away from the seductive clutches of Bataille. Crevel, Eluard and Breton tried to reclaim the 'paranoiac-critical thought' theorized by Dalí, whereas Aragon remained more cautious. Lacan and Dalí inspired each other to refine the concept of paranoia.

Breton at the first Dalí exhibition

Dalí here is like a man who hesitates (and whom the future will show did not hesitate) between talent and genius – in another age one would have said between vice and virtue. He is one of those who arrive from far enough away that in order to see them enter – and only enter – one should not have the time to see them. He sets himself, without saying a word, within a system of interferences.... The action that we have brought against reality is one which we are completely convinced we shall win, and that is why from now on we intend – by surrounding him with a special splendour – to produce the pathetic testimony of a man who seems to us of all men to have nothing to save: nothing, not even his head. With us alive, no matter what may happen, no one will plant the ignoble flag of the motherland, of art, or even of defeat in Cimmeria, the solitary place that we have discovered anew and that we intend to reserve for ourselves. Dalí, who reigns over these distant lands, is to be instructed by examples too numerous and too reprehensible for him to let himself be dispossessed of his marvellous country of treasures. May it please the mighty, of whom he is the envoy in this world, that he should for ever keep his eyes closed to the wretched plans for bridges which greed and spite will do their utmost to make him throw over the brilliant, unapproachable and magnetic river....

André Breton, 'Point du jour', 1929,
from *Oeuvres Complètes I*, Paris, 1988

Bataille and *The Lugubrious Game*

...I have to say, virtually without preamble, that the paintings of Picasso are hideous, and those of Dalí are of an appalling ugliness. One is a victim of the inadequacy of words, or indeed of an evil spell somewhat redolent of the practices of black magic when one assures oneself of the contrary. It is enough merely to imagine the little girl, of charming appearance, whose soul is the abominable mirror of Dalí, to measure the extent of the evil. The tongue of this little girl is not a tongue but a female rat. And if she still seems admirably beautiful, it is because – as people say – black blood is beautiful, running over the coat of an ox or the throat of a woman....

In everything there is a gradual revelation of contradictory signs of servitude and revolt. After all is said and done, the great constructions of intelligence are prisons: that is why they are stubbornly reversed. The dreams and the illusory Cimmerias remain within the reach of dyed-in-the-wool ditherers, whose unconscious tactic is not so dumb because they innocently place their revolt under the protection of laws. Besides, how can one not admire the loss of will, the blind allure, the uncertainty of drifting from permitted distraction to attention? It is true that I am speaking here of that which already falls into oblivion when Dalí's razors cut into our very own faces grimaces of horror that probably risk making us vomit out like drunkards that servile nobility, that idiotic idealism that left us under the spell of some comic prison warders.

Georges Bataille, 'Le *Jeu Lugubre*' in *Documents*, no. 7, December 1929

Salvador Dalí, flanked by André Breton and René Crevel.

Review slip for Dalí's *La Femme Visible*, by Eluard and Breton

The miserable mental expedient that hides behind the words 'the reality' makes our time into an object of systematic denunciation, whose revolutionary consequences are indisputable. In fact it is a matter of demonstrating – and Surrealism has no other aspiration – that reasons of social conservation, based on individual cowardice, are at the origin of the very assailable phenomenon of voluntary amnesia on which man leans in order to try and deceive others as well as himself about the true character of his desires.

In 1930 it falls to Dalí more than to any other to take man out of this cavern of lies which, with the connivance of unnameable public powers he is building up around himself, and to make him aware firstly and lastly that he is a being who comes from non-being and returns there, but returns there without the useless baseness related to a transitory organic condition.

Depending today on Dalí's great gifts – gifts defined on the level of art – is the destruction of an outmoded formula which is, one is persuaded, that of a bourgeois world reduced to using for its armed defence the ever sharper – as a consequence of its being ever more breakable – weapon of censorship.

Dialectical thought combined with psychoanalytical thought, each crowning the other with what Dalí in such striking manner calls paranoiac-critical thought, is the most admirable instrument that has yet been proposed for driving into immortal ruins the phantom woman with verdigris face…who is not only the spirit of our birth, that is to say of Art Nouveau, but is also the ever more alluring phantom of the future.

From André Breton, 'Alentours III', in *Oeuvres Complètes I*, 'Bibliothèque de la Pléiade', Paris, 1988

Aragon's view of the collage

What may most defy interpretation is Salvador Dalí's use of collage. He paints with a magnifying glass; he is able to imitate a print to the point at which the effect is guaranteed: the collaged sections of the print pass for paint, while the painted sections pass for collage. Is this an attempt to puzzle the eye, and does it give him pleasure to create this deception? One might think so, but one will not find an explanation of this double game, which cannot be attributed to the painter's despair when faced with the inimitable, or to his laziness when faced with the fact that everything has already been expressed. It is also certain that the incoherent aspects of Dalí's picture, in its ensemble, recall the incoherence that is special to collages. Earlier attempts have been made to reduce Max Ernst's collages to plastic poems. If for psychological ends one wished to sketch out a similar sort of manoeuvre with regard to Dalí's paintings, one would have to pretend that each of his pictures is a novel. In this context too, Dalí associates himself with the anti-pictorial spirit that quite recently elicited cries from the painters and then from the critics, and which today is taking over painting. This is what is to be retained of this sequence of facts at which we are present and which could seem chaotic to anyone who cannot see the essential link.

Louis Aragon, *La Peinture au Défi*, Paris, 1930

Crevel and anti-obscurantism

...Dalí undoubtedly has prodigious gifts of expression at his disposal, but these gifts collectively do not in any way constitute the mosaic of vocations that traditional psychology would certainly like to point to, in order to show that the time of the Pico della Mirandolas is not definitively and irrevocably over, as one might fear.

Without searching for comparisons in the Italian Renaissance or elsewhere, if Dalí is at one and the same time painter, sculptor, poet, philosopher and orator of unmatchably direct eloquence, if he has collaborated with Luis Buñuel on *Un Chien Andalou* and *L'Age d'Or*, the first and only two subversive films, it is because painting (and to hell with the art critics who condemn because it is literary the art which does not accept being bestially greedy), the art of sculpting, poetizing, screenwriting, and the art of making oneself heard by ideological specialists or at public meetings, are not ends but means....

The right of thought to paranoia, no matter what our Mussolinis of mental hygiene may say about it, is the same as the right of a penis to have an erection and to ejaculate. But let's have no more covers over objects, no more French letters over ideas. The condoms stretch and break, these protections against pleasure, these spider's webs against danger.

At the time of sleep, Breton wrote: 'Words, words in the end make love.' Today, if it is said that objects stretch, this is by no means a metaphorical caprice. And they do not stretch at random. They caress one another, suck one another, devour one another, make love! – these surreal objects that Dalí thought up and whose opportunities, resources and erotic suggestiveness he devised, to see in action that ball of wood which Giacometti marked with a female hollow so that it could slide onto the ridge of a long fruit of the same material but in manly form, each of them at the end of their tether, crazy about each other, and each making the other share this mode of effect with those that looked on them, which *a priori* would scarcely have seemed possible for two pieces of smooth boxwood, but which became indisputable thanks to the fact that a piece of string holding the ball back in its passion did not allow it to fall into the nirvana of satisfaction.

René Crevel, 'Dalí ou l'Anti-Obscurantisme', in *L'Esprit contre la Raison*, Paris, 1986

Breton's view of the paranoiac method

One must (in order to give a basic idea of Dalí's work) indulge in passionate speculation on this quality of uninterrupted becoming in every object exposed to the paranoiac activity, or in other words the ultra-confusional activity that has its source in the obsessive idea. This uninterrupted becoming allows the paranoiac who witnesses it to take the images even of my exterior as unstable and transient, if not suspect, and it is – this is disturbing – within its power to control in others the reality of the impression that it makes. For example, a condition of the multiple image that occupies our attention might be a rotten donkey, with the 'cruel' putrefaction of the donkey being maintained for 'the blinding and harsh reflection of new precious stones'. Here we find ourselves in the presence of a new declaration, backed up by formal evidence, of the omnipotence of desire which, from the beginning, has remained the sole article of the Surrealist faith. At the point at which Surrealism discovered the problem, let us remember that its only reference had been Rimbaud's sibylline watchword:

'I say that one must be conspicuous, make oneself conspicuous.'

André Breton, 'Qu'est-ce que le surréalisme?', 1934, in *Oeuvres Complètes II*, Paris, 1992

The most recent trends in Surrealist painting, by Breton

…It is worth noting that of the painters who have most recently appeared on the scene – though of their predecessors I would regard Paulen, who has long since demonstrated his mastery, as an exception – the modern influence exercised in most determinate fashion is that of Tanguy. By contrast, that of Dalí marks a very rapid decline. It could not be otherwise, seeing that his taste for giving pleasure is pushed to the point of paroxysm, making it necessary for him to constantly exceed his own paradoxes. In February 1939 Dalí declared – I have this from his own lips, and I have taken the time to ascertain that any kind of humour is excluded from this proposition – that all the present troubles of the world are racial, and that the solution that needs to prevail, through a concerted effort by all the people of white race, is to reduce all coloured people to slavery. I do not know what doors such a declaration will open for its author in Italy and the United States, countries between which he commutes, but I know what doors it will close for him. After this I do not see how one can continue to take account of his message in independent circles. Already profound and utter monotony is posing a threat to Dalí's painting. In his efforts to refine his paranoiac method, one can see that he is beginning to slide into an entertainment akin to crossword puzzles.

André Breton, in *Minotaure*, nos. 12–13, Paris, 1939

Beyond painting

The desire to escape from the limitations of painting in order to better communicate the Surrealist experience, led Dalí to follow Breton's example in creating paradoxical objects that were designed to spread greater confusion in the world of reality. From the object to the environment and to architecture, via the cinema, Dalí set out to 'conquer the irrational'.

Surrealist objects exhibited

Object by Gala Eluard
Two metallic antennae, oscillating, curved.

At their ends, two sponges, one metallic and the other natural, shaped in the form of breasts, and to designate the nipples, small bones in carmine. When the antennae are set in motion, one of the above-mentioned sponges brushes against a bowl of flour, and the other against the spiky bristles of a metal brush. The bowl itself is installed in a box set at an angle and containing other objects that correspond to additional representations. A red membrane, which is elastic and remains mobile for a long time after the slightest movement, with a small, black, flexible spring resembling an ankle hangs down from a little red cage. A brush of white wood and a pharmaceutical glass tube divide the compartments of the box.

Object by Salvador Dalí
A woman's shoe, inside which a glass of warm milk has been placed, at the centre of a paste of ductile form and excremental colour.

The mechanism consists of dipping a lump of sugar on which has been painted the image of a shoe, so that one can observe the disintegration of the sugar and, as a consequence, the image of the shoe in the milk. Several accessories (pubic hairs stuck to a piece of sugar, a small erotic photo) complete the object, which is accompanied by a box of spare sugar cubes and a special spoon that is used to stir granules of lead inside the shoe.

Salvador Dalí, 'Objets Surréalistes, Catalogue', in *Surréalisme au Service de la Révolution*, nos. 3–4, Paris, 1931

'The Object as Revealed in Surrealist Experiment'

...The early surrealist experimenters found themselves plunged into the subterranean passages of 'Revolution by Night', the passages where *The Mysteries of New York* must have just been enacted, in fact, dream passages still identifiable today. They found themselves plunged in the post-mechanical open street, where the most beautiful and hallucinating iron vegetation sprouts those electric blooms still decorating in the 'Modern Style' the entrances to the Paris Métro. There they were stricken with oblivion and, owing to the threat of unintended cataclysms, became highly developed automatic puppets such as men now risk becoming. All night long, a few surrealists would gather round the big table used for experiments, their eyes protected and masked by thin though opaque mechanical slats on which the blinding curve of the convulsive graphs would appear intermittently in fleeting luminous signals, a delicate nickel apparatus like an astrolabe being fixed to their necks and fitted with animal membranes to record by interpenetration the apparition of each fresh poetic streak, their bodies being bound to their chairs by an ingenious system of straps, so that they could only move a hand in a certain way and the sinuous line was allowed to inscribe the appropriate white cylinders. Meanwhile their friends, holding their breath and biting their lower lips in concentrated attention, would lean over the recording apparatus and with dilated pupils await the expected but unknown movement, sentence, or image.

On the table, a few scientific instruments employed in a system of physics now forgotten or still to be elaborated, endowed the night with their different temperatures and the different smells of their delicate mechanisms, having been made a little feverish by the fresh and cool taste of the electricity. There was also a woman's bronze glove and several other perverted articles such as 'that kind of white, irregular, varnished, half-cylinder with apparently meaningless bulges and hollows,' which is mentioned in *Nadja*, and, further, the cage Breton describes in *Wandering Footsteps*: 'I have in mind the occasion when Marcel Duchamp got hold of

some friends to show them a cage which seemed to have no birds in it, but to be half-full of lumps of sugar. He asked them to lift the cage and they were surprised at its heaviness. What they had taken for lumps of sugar were really small lumps of marble which at great expense Duchamp had had sawn up specially for the purpose. The trick in my opinion is no worse than any other, and I would even say that it is worth nearly all the tricks of art put together.'

Salvador Dalí, 'The Object as Revealed in Surrealist Experiment', from *This Quarter*, 5(1), Paris, September 1932 (originally published in English, translation by David Gascoyne)

Edible architecture

…I believe that I was the first in 1929 and at the beginning of *The Visible Woman* to consider, without a trace of humour, delirious Modern Style architecture as the most original and the most extraordinary phenomenon in art history.

Here I insist on the essentially extra-plastic character of the Modern Style. All utilization of this for genuinely 'plastic' or pictorial ends would definitely be regarded by me as the most flagrant treason against the irrationalist and basically 'literary' aspirations of this movement. The 'replacement' (a question of fatigue) of the formula 'right angle' and 'golden section' by the convulsive-undulating formula can in the long run only give rise to an aestheticism as sad as its predecessor – temporarily less boring as a result of the change, but that is all. The best people claim to represent this formula: the curved line today seems once more to have become the shortest, most vertiginous route from one point to another – only all that is nothing but the 'death throes of plasticism'. Anti-decorative decorativism, in contrast to the psychic decorativism of the Modern Style....

It is in architecture that we shall be able to admire the profound shock, in essence the most consubstantially functionalist, to every 'element' – whether the most congenital or the most hereditary – of the past. With the Modern Style, the architectural elements of the past, apart from the fact that they will be submitted to a frequent and total, convulsive-formal grinding-up that will give birth to a new stylization, will be called upon to come back to life and to survive in the present beneath their true and original aspect, in such a manner that by combining with one another, by merging with one another (despite their intellectually most irreconcilable, most irreducible differences) they will attain the highest degree of aesthetic depreciation, and will manifest in their relationships that dreadful impurity whose only equivalent and equal is the immaculate purity of dream-like intertwinings.

In a modern-style building, the Gothic is metamorphosed into the Hellenic, into the Far Eastern, and if it passes at all through the head, through a certain involuntary fantasy, into the Renaissance, which in turn may become pure, dynamic-asymmetrical (!) modern style, all of this in the 'feeble' time and space of a single window – that is to say, in the little-known and probably vertiginous time and space which, as we have just hinted, will be none other than those of the dream.

All that has been most naturally utilitarian and functionalist in the known architectures of the past, suddenly no longer serves any purpose at all in the Modern Style, or that which cannot win over pragmatic intellectualism no longer serves any purpose but the 'functioning of desires' which moreover are the most disturbed, discredited and shameful.

Salvador Dalí, 'De la Beauté Terrifiante et Comestible de l'Architecture Modern Style', in *Minotaure*, nos. 3–4, Paris, 1933

The phenomenon of ecstasy

Ecstasy constitutes the most phenomenally overwhelming *élan vital* of spectres and psychic representations. – During ecstasy, with the onset of desire, of pleasure, of anguish, every opinion, every judgment (moral, aesthetic, etc.) changes sensationally. – Every image too changes sensationally. One might think that through ecstasy we gain access to a world that is as distant from reality as that of the dream. – The repugnant can be transformed into the desirable, affection into cruelty, ugliness into beauty, defects into qualities, qualities into black miseries. – Ecstasy is the culminating consequence of dreams, it is the consequence and the mortal verification of the images of our perversion. – Some images create ecstasy, which in turn creates other images. – This has always been a matter of images authentically and essentially surrealistic. – Ecstasy is the 'pure state' of exigent and hyperaesthetic, vital lucidity, the blind lucidity of desire. – The world of images aroused by ecstasy is infinite and unknown. – These are neologistic images, images that are extra swift by comparison with hypnagogic images. – Any methodology to deal with this subject has so far escaped us. – Sometimes the images aroused by ecstasy repeat transfigured images of ecstasy, whether they are the 'apparent'

stereotype of the ears (these are always in ecstasy), or the ecstasy of a certain 'atmospheric thing', or the refined ecstasy of a Modern Style needle.
– I ask the art critic: what would you think of such and such a work at the moment of your ecstasy? And first of all: get yourself in a state of ecstasy in order to answer me. – Ecstasy is *par excellence* the critical mental state which the fantastic current, hysterical, modern Surrealistic and phenomenal thought aspires to make 'continuous'. – In search of images that are likely to put us into the state of ecstasy.

Salvador Dalí, 'De la Beauté Terrifiante et Comestible de l'Architecture Modern Style', in *Minotaure*, nos. 3–4, Paris, 1933

Film art, the anti-artistic thread

The artistic director, corrupted by the indigestible absorption of literature and with a risible desire for originality, tends to favour a maximum of complexity and expressive, psychological conflicts, which he combines with the widest, most varied assortment of recourses, very often extra-cinematographical, all of which leads of course directly to the anecdote, which has all the appearance of transcendentalism but at bottom is perfectly innocent and puerile. The anonymous anti-artistic director films a white confection, some sort of room, innocuous and simple, the guard's van, the policeman's star, a kiss in a taxi. Once the film is shown, we know that what has been filmed is a whole world of unimaginably poetic fairy tales. Fritz Lang stages a grand spectacle: architects, engineers, very bright, intersecting spotlights, grandiose Dantean sets, proportions called grandiose, where crowds, lights, machines are swarming…with all the

Figueras, 1929

Salvador Dalí (centre) with Luis Buñuel and his sister Ana María, Figueras, 1929.

worst theatricality of historical painting. That a Moreno Carbonero paints the Middle Ages or a skyscraper is not the same thing. This kind of cinema becomes a medium of expression for the most spurious and vulgar anecdote; the pure, newborn thrill of it is appallingly infected by all the germs of artistic putrefaction.

Salvador Dalí, in *Gaceta Literaria*, 15 December 1927, article dedicated to Luis Buñuel

Dalí–Lorca, an uncompromising friendship

The painter and the poet, both students in Madrid, experienced a passionate friendship, in which tokens of affection fulfilled the double demands of aesthetics and philosophy. Dalí responded to Lorca's 'Ode to Salvador Dalí' with a text on St Sebastian – emblem of the modern artist, and passive recipient of sensory impressions. These themes were pursued through an intense correspondence, in which intellectual exchanges were coupled with allusions to an impossible love.

Ode to Salvador Dalí

A rose in the high garden you desire
A wheel in the pure syntax of steel
The mountain stripped of impressionist
  fog
The greys looking down over their last
  balustrades
The modern painters in their white
  studios
Cut the aseptic flower of the square root
In the waters of the Seine, a marble
  iceberg
Chills the windows and scatters the ivy....
Sailors who know nothing of wine
  or twilight
Decapitate mermaids on the seas of lead
The Night, black statue of prudence,
  holds
The round mirror of the moon
  in her hand
A desire for forms and limits takes
  us over
Here comes the man who watches
  with the yellow rule
Venus is a white still life

And the butterfly collectors flee
Cadaqués on the fulcrum of the
  water and the hill
Lifts staircases and hides seashells
Wooden flutes pacify the air
An old rustic god gives fruits to children
Her fishermen sleep dreamlessly
  on the sand
On the high seas, their compass is a rose
The horizon free of wounded
  handkerchiefs
Joins the great windows of the fish
  and the moon
A hard crown of white brigantines
Encircles bitter foreheads and hair
  of sand
The mermaids convince, but they
  do not enchant
And they come when we show them
  a glass of fresh water
O Salvador Dalí, with your olive voice
I do not praise your imperfect
  adolescent brush
Or your colour that courts the colours
  of your time

But I hail your longing for eternal limits
Hygienic soul, you live on new marble
You flee the dark forest of incredible
  forms
Your fantasy goes where your hands go
And you enjoy the sonnet of the sea at
  your window
The world holds muffled darkness
  and disorder
In the foreground where humans tread
But the stars, hiding landscapes,
Now reveal the perfect plan of their
  orbits...
When you pick up your palette, shot
  in one wing
You call on the light that brings the olive
  grove to life
The broad light of Minerva, builder
  of scaffolding
Where there is no space for sleep or its
  vague flowers...
You do well to post warning flags
along the dark frontier that shines
  in the night.
As a painter you do not want your form
  softened
by the changing cotton of an unexpected
  cloud...
You love matter that is defined and exact
Where no fungus could make its camp
You love architecture built in the absent
And you accept the flag like a simple
  joke
The steel compass speaks its short elastic
  verse
Unknown islands are denied by the
  globe
The straight line describes its vertical
  thrust
And the wise crystals sing their
  geometries.
But also the rose in the garden where
  you live
Forever the rose, for always, north and
  south of us!
Calm and concentrated like a blind statue,

Knowing nothing of the buried struggle
  it causes
Pure rose that cleans away artifice
  and sketches
And opens to us the delicate wings
  of a smile
(Pinned butterfly that ponders its flight)
Rose of balance, without sought-out
  sorrows
Forever the rose!...
Do not watch the water clock with its
  membrane wings
Nor the tough scythe of allegory.
Forever dress and undress your brush
  in the air
Facing the sea filled with boats
  and sailors.

Federico García Lorca, 1926

Letters of impossible love

Cadaqués, early summer 1926
I'll talk to you once more about
St Objectivity, which is now called
St Sebastian.

Cadaqués is a 'sufficient fact', and
to talk of surpassing it would be an
exaggeration, a venial sin; excessive
profundity could also be worse, it could
be ecstasy. As for me, I do not like things
that give me extraordinary pleasure; I
flee from things through which I would
risk going into ecstasy, just as I flee from
cars; ecstasy is a danger to intelligence.

It is seven o'clock, when I stop
painting, at the time when the sky is
capable of extraordinary and dangerous
things – it is at this time that instead
of contemplating the almost unbearable
spectacle of nature, I take my Charleston
lessons at the Salisacs'; the dance is
very respectable, because it is a perfect
impoverishment of the mind, and
I really feel good! I am in full Easter
resurrection! The fact of not feeling
the anguish of wanting to give oneself
totally; this nightmare of feeling oneself
plunging into nature, that is to say into
the mystery, into something confused,
something ungraspable, at last to be
sitting down, limited to a few truths,
a few preferences, clear, orderly, and
sufficient for my spiritual sensitivity.

Monsieur the professor tells me: but
nature too possesses its order, its laws,
its superior measures. 'Superior' – a
dangerous word, which means superior
to us, an order incomprehensible to us,
laws and mysterious measures, and there
we are into religion, and we enter into
the principles of faith and
obscurantism....

But thank God, today one knows
exactly where art begins and where
naturism begins.

Goethe, that great thinker, has already
said that nature and art are two different
things. Le Corbusier knows a lot about
this field and also about love.

Letter from Dalí to Lorca, from
*Salvador Dalí Escribe a Federico García
Lorca*, ed. Rafael Santos Torroella,
Madrid, 1987

September 1928

In reality there is no relation between
two dancers and a honeycomb, unless it
is the relation that exists between Saturn
and the little caterpillar asleep in the
chrysalis, or unless in reality there is no
difference between the dancing couple
and a honeycomb.

The minute hand (don't keep an
account of my examples – I don't exactly
hunt for poetic ones) only acquires any
real value when it ceases to indicate the
hours and, during its circular rhythm
and its arbitrary mission to which our
intelligence has subjected it (indicating
the hours), escapes from the watch in
order to place itself at the spot which
would correspond to the genitals of the
little crumbs of bread.

As for you, you evolve in the sphere
of ideas, permissible and antipoetic.
You talk of a cavalier, and according to
you that implies that he is on a horse and
the horse is galloping; that is saying a
lot, because in reality one should
confirm if it actually is the cavalier up
there, and if the reins are not an organic
continuation of the hands themselves,
and if in reality the little hairs on the
balls of the cavalier are not travelling
faster than the horse, and one should
see if the horse is not, on the contrary,
stationary, fixed to the ground by sturdy
roots…and so on and so on. Think a
little about what it is to go from there, as
you do, to the concept of a civil guard.
To tell the truth, speaking poetically,

a civil guard doesn't exist, unless he's a sweet, merry figure, lively and brilliant, simply by virtue of his qualities and the little horns of his cap sticking out all over, and his little straps and belts which form a visceral part of this little beast, and so on and so on.

But you…in keeping with the norms of putrefaction – the civil guard – what does he do? such, such, such irreality, irreality. – Anti-poetry – abstract concept of things: one must liberate the little things from the conventional ideas to which intelligence has tried to subject them – Well, these pretty little things act alone, in accordance with their real and consubstantial way of being – Let them decide for themselves on the direction in which they project their shadows! and it may be that the thing whose extended shadow we imagined does not make any, and so on and so on. Ugly, beautiful? Words that no longer have any meaning. Horror, that's something else, that's what knowledge of reality inspires in us, far from all aesthetics, since lyricism is not possible except in the framework of our intelligence's more or less approximate perceptions of reality.

Last letter from Dalí to Lorca, from Ian Gibson, *Lorca, Dalí: El Amor Que No Pudo Ser*, Barcelona, 1999

Leaving Cadaqués, July 1927
It makes me enthusiastic just to think what discoveries you are going to make in Cadaqués, and I remember the neophyte Salvador licking the shell of the twilight without entering it, the pale pink carapace of the overturned crab. Today you are inside. From here I can sense (ouch, my son, what a pity!) the sweet little rain of the girlfriend bleeding in a wood of apparatuses, and I can hear two little beasts crackling like the sound of peanuts which you open between your fingers. The divided woman is the finest poem that one can make on the subject of blood, and which contains more blood than all that flowed in the European War, which was warm blood whose aim was to water the earth and to quench a thirst, symbol of eroticism and faith. Your pictorial blood and, in general, the whole plastic concept of your physiological aesthetics possesses a concrete air that is so well proportioned, so logical, and so true – as pure poetry is – that it attains the status of that which we need in order to live.

One might say, 'I was more and more tired, and I sat down in the shade and in the freshness of this blood,' or again, 'I went down the hill and I ran along the beach to look for the melancholy head around which were grouped once more the delicious crackling beasts that are so necessary for good digestion.'

Now I know what I am losing by parting from you. The impression Barcelona gives me is that everyone is playing and sweating, worrying about oblivion. Everything is confused and menacing, like the aesthetics of the flame, everything is indecisive and distracted. Over there in Cadaqués people set all the twists and all the pores of the soles of their feet on the ground. I see now just how aware I was of my shoulders in Cadaqués. It is a delight to recall the sliding curves of my shoulders where, for the first time, I felt the blood circulating inside four spongy little tubes that trembled with the movements of the wounded swimmer.

Letter from Lorca to Dalí, from Ian Gibson, *Lorca, Dalí: El Amor Que No Pudo Ser*, Barcelona, 1999

Biography and autobiography

Dalí's awareness of the power of self-image and instinct for self-promotion were overridingly strong and finely controlled throughout the various stages of his life. His own autobiographical writings in particular, such as Diary of a Genius, *although filled with paradoxes, half-truths and traps, should not prevent us from savouring the humour and the wit, the mischievousness and sometimes even the tenderness that they contain.*

Dalí's multiple selves

For almost forty years, Dalí [was] one of the two most famous painters alive. As a bodily trademark, his moustache was the only rival to van Gogh's ear and Picasso's testicles; though unlike them, it was adopted from Velásquez's portrait of Philip IV. Dalí's success, large as it was, coincided with his decline as a serious artist. Painters often imitate themselves (and certainly Miró's late work, most of it reflexively churned out to satisfy the demands of the market, is no exception), but Dalí did so with unusual zeal, and his celebrity arises from the way in which he fulfilled two ruling clichés about artists. The first was the Painter as Old Master (Raphael, Rubens); the second, the Artist as Freak (Rimbaud, van Gogh). Dalí's public image contrived to give a tacky, vivid caricature of both while fulfilling neither. Here, on one hand, was early Dalí: a manic and unrestrained imagination, immersed in sovereign private fantasy. On the other, the late Dalí convinced an audience that could scarcely tell the difference between

a Vermeer and a Velásquez that he was the spiritual heir to both painters. He did both, not so much through art as by the diffusion of small anecdotes and a stoic indifference to the pangs of self-repetition. 'The difference between a madman and me,' Dalí is often quoted as saying, 'is that I am not mad.' Indeed he is not; and in his later years, the Catalan promoter, with his moustache-wax, lobster-telephones, and soft watches, managed to annihilate his earlier self – crazy Sal the Andalusian Dog, the insecure and ravenously aggressive young dandy whose tiny, enamelled visions helped create one of the extreme moments of modernist disgust and revolt.

...As Picasso used his erotic rage as a subject throughout his life, Dalí deployed an imagery of impotence and guilt. He liked anything that was not erect, that spoke of flaccidity – runny Camembert cheese, Gaudí's stonework, melon-like lobes of flesh held up by crutches, soft watches, fried eggs, deliquescent heads. He inherited from Spanish devotional art...an alm ost paralyzing morbidity about flesh. In Dalí it suffers, scourged by light, and seems ripe as over-hung grouse: there is no such thing as the confident body, but no spiritual transcendence of the flesh either. Hence the peculiarly airless, pessimistic tone of Dalí's work, another characteristic that it, like much Surrealist art, shared with pornography.

Robert Hughes, *The Shock of the New*, London, 1980

Surrealism in the city

Bread was...the theme around which Dalí built one of his elaborate campaigns, in the early thirties, related to the Surrealist object. He wanted to bake a loaf fifteen metres long, for which a special oven would have to be constructed. This bread would then be deposited at some comparatively unfrequented spot, like the gardens of the Palais Royal, without any indication as to who had made it or why. The bread would then be discovered as an 'insoluble fact' in the heart of Paris; a few days later it would be followed by another loaf twenty metres long, and this in turn by others culminating in the appearance of a new loaf of French bread forty-five metres long lying on the sidewalk in New York, edible ancestor of Claes Oldenburg's huge soft city monuments, and a potential advertising stunt par excellence. Dalí is, of course, here playing games with the original notion of the Surrealist object's manifest purposelessness throwing discredit on the ordinary functional objects of the real world, because the sense of confusion comes in this case from the reverse, from the introduction of the most practical object of all into a context alien to it and in a vastly exaggerated dimension. Dalí's purpose is to sow confusion, as he explained rather cynically in *The Secret Life*: 'No one would be able to question the efficacy of such an act which in itself would be capable of creating a state of confusion, of panic and of collective hysteria extremely instructive from an experimental point of view and capable of becoming a point of departure from which, according to my principles of the imaginative hierarchical monarchy, one could subsequently try to ruin systematically the logical meaning of all the mechanisms of the rational practical world.'

...Dalí from the late thirties tended to favour the creation of whole environments and objects on a monumental scale, often with a highly theatrical flavour. In 1939, for example, he created a pavilion for the New York World's Fair, with the assistance of his New York dealer Julien Levy. The installation, baptized *The Dream of Venus*, was to be on a stand in the Amusement Area of the fair, and was to consist of a giant water tank to be filled with both real and model sirens, various other objects (a man made of rubber ping-pong bats), a Surrealist landscape backcloth with soft watches, and huge reproductions of the *Mona Lisa* and Botticelli's *Birth of Venus*. It was not, in the end, according to Levy, a complete success, because of the problems of getting the 'middlemen', in this case those putting up the money for the installation, to agree to Dalí's more extravagant suggestions: extravagant, that is, in terms of the imagination rather than money. One promoter, a rubber manufacturer, wanted, against furious resistance from Dalí, to fill the tank with rubber mermaids, in Dalí's understandable opinion a banal and second-rate idea. He was in turn horrified by Dalí's plan to have Botticelli's *Venus* on a vast scale on the facade, with a fish's head. He complained to the organizing committee, who prohibited it, and thus provoked Dalí to write a spirited parody of the Americal Declaration of the Rights of Man: 'Declaration of the Independence of the Imagination and of the Rights of Man to his Own Madness'....

It was Levy who set up another project, the same year, which ended in one of Dalí's involuntary news-catching escapades. He arranged for Dalí to do a window dressing for the Bonwit-Teller store on Fifth Avenue, and, as he says, 'Dalí was enchanted by the rich prospect of realizing his inventions in this workshop.' Dalí set up a window which included a bath-tub with a mannequin reclining inside; unfortunately, overnight the mannequin was moved out of the bath by a zealous employee to give a better view of its gown. Dalí flew into a rage when he saw his idea ruined, and in the resulting mêlée he and the bath-tub crashed through the window into the Avenue. Dalí was arrested pending criminal charges of wilful destruction, but was released later the same day. He certainly had not intended this as a publicity stunt, but the effect was that he was confirmed in the public eye as the most outrageous artist of the time.

Dawn Ades, *Dalí*, revised edition, London, 1995

Diary of a Genius

1 May 1952

When the Surrealists discovered in my father's house in Cadaqués the picture which I had just finished painting and which Paul Eluard baptized *The Lugubrious Game*, they were scandalized by the scatological and anal elements in the image depicted. Gala especially disapproved of my work with a vehemence that appalled me that day but which, since then, I have learned to adore. I was about to enter the Surrealist group whose watchwords and subjects I had just been conscientiously studying, dissecting them right down to the tiniest bone. I thought I had understood that one had to spontaneously transcribe thought without any rational, aesthetic or moral control. However, before I even effectively and with the best will in the world entered the group, they were going to impose upon me constraints that were similar to those of my own family. Gala was the first to warn me that among the Surrealists I would suffer the same vetoes as elsewhere, and that at heart they were all bourgeois. My power, she predicted, would lie in remaining equidistant from all artistic and literary movements. With an intuition which surpassed even my own, she added that the originality of my paranoiac-critical method of analysis would have been enough for any member of the group to start a separate school....

The Surrealist group was convened one evening to pass judgment on my alleged Hitlerism. This session, most details of which I have unfortunately forgotten, was extraordinary.... While I was pleading my cause, I knelt down several times, not in order to beg that I should not be expelled – as has been falsely reported – but, on the contrary, to urge Breton to understand that my obsession with Hitler was strictly paranoiac and essentially apolitical. I also explained to them that I could not be a Nazi, because if Hitler conquered Europe, he would make the most of it by ensuring that all hysterics of my ilk would be destroyed, as had already been done in Germany by treating them as degenerates. And finally, the feminine and irresistibly crazy role that I attributed to Hitler's character would have been enough to make the Nazis classify me as an iconoclast…. At last they were convinced of my innocence, but all the same I had to sign a document in which, among other things, I declared that I was not an enemy of the proletariat.

27 July 1952
This morning, an exceptional defecation: two small stools in the form of rhinoceros horns. Such a meagre bowel movement worries me. I should have thought that champagne, to which I am so little accustomed, would have had a laxative effect. But less than an hour afterwards, I had to go to the lavatory again, where at last I had a normal bowel movement. My two rhinoceros horns were therefore the end of another process. I shall return to this question, which is of primordial interest….

18 December 1955
Dalinian apotheosis yesterday evening in the Temple of Knowledge before a fascinated congregation…. The trembling audience expected some decisive words. They got them…. In order to confirm my utterances, the image was projected of a copy that I had made of a painting by Raphael, clearly influenced by my rhinocerotic obsessions. This painting – a crucifixion – is one of the greatest examples of the conical organization of a surface. It was not, I specified, the horn of a rhinoceros such as one finds in Vermeer (where it has a far greater potency) – no, it was the horn of a rhinoceros that could be called neoplatonic…. Once more my audience gasped. I bombarded them with other blunt truths. The projector showed them the photo of a rhinoceros's

arse, which I had recently analysed with great subtlety, making the discovery that it was nothing other than a sunflower folded in two. The rhinoceros is not content with bearing one of the most beautiful logarithmic curves on the end of its nose, but also in its rear it bears a kind of galaxy of logarithmic curves in the form of a sunflower…. After studying the morphology of the sunflower, I said, I felt that its points, its curves, and its shadows had a taciturn air that corresponds perfectly to the profound melancholy of Leonardo da Vinci himself. I asked myself the question: was it not too mechanical? The sunflower's mask of dynamism prevented me from seeing *The Lacemaker* in the sunflower. I was studying the question when suddenly by chance I stumbled on the photo of a cauliflower…Revelation: the morphological problem of the cauliflower is identical to that of the sunflower in the sense that it too is made up of true logarithmic spirals. But the flowering has a kind of expansive force, almost a nuclear force. A burgeoning tension similar to the stubborn, meningitic brow that I love so passionately in *The Lacemaker*. I had come to the Sorbonne in a Rolls packed with vegetables, but it was not the season for giant cauliflowers. One must wait till next March. The biggest that I can find I shall light and photograph at a certain angle. Then – and I gave my word of honour as a Spaniard – once the photo has been developed, everyone will see in it a *Lacemaker* with the actual technique of Vermeer. The hall was filled with an absolute frenzy!

Salvador Dalí, *Journal d'un Génie*, 'L'Imaginaire', Paris, 1996

MUSEUM COLLECTIONS

Some of the public collections that hold important works by Salvador Dalí:

The MOMA (Museum of Modern Art) in New York, the first museum to hold a Dalí retrospective, in 1942, was also the first to have acquired a Dalí work (1934) – the famous soft watches in *The Persistence of Memory*, bought by Julien Levy in Paris in June 1931. Also to be seen there are *The Angelus of Gala* (1935), *Study of Horsemen* (1936), and *Debris of a Car Giving Birth to a Blind Horse Biting a Telephone* (1938).

A. Reynolds and Eleanor R. Morse discovered Dalí's work at the MOMA retrospective when it was shown in Cleveland in 1942, and began their long career as purchasers and patrons, which continued until Dalí died. Their entire collection – one of the finest, extending from 1917 until 1970 – has been on display since 1982 in Saint Petersburg, Florida, initially in old warehouses and then in the present Salvador Dalí Museum, which houses 95 oil paintings, 100 watercolours and drawings, 1,300 sketches, photographs, sculptures, objects and an archive.

Donations that Dalí made during his lifetime to the Spanish State provided the Museo Nacional Centro de Arte Reina Sofía in Madrid with several important pictures, and these were followed by purchases which included his masterpiece *The Great Masturbator* (1929). Another Spanish institution to have benefited from donations by

Dalí is the Dalí Theatre Museum of Figueras, managed by the Gala-Salvador Dalí Foundation, which also runs the Salvador Dalí House-Museum in Port Lligat and the Chateau Gala Dalí House-Museum in Púbol. Nearly 4,000 works are to be seen there, including many drawings and archives. The Foundation, which controls the rights to Dalí's work, has for some years been carrying out a dynamic programme of acquisitions and publications.

The Musée National d'Art Moderne at the Centre Pompidou in Paris owns several Dalí paintings connected with Dalí's time in the city – including *The Spectral Cow* (1928) and *Sometimes I Take Pleasure in Spitting on the Portrait of My Mother* (first displayed at the Goemans exhibition in 1929) – or with the Parisian history of the Surrealist movement, including *Invisible Sleeper, Horse and Lion* (1930) and what the French regard as Dalí's most famous painting: *Partial Hallucination, Six Images of Lenin on a Piano* (1931). The museum's Cabinet des Dessins owns many drawings, including *Cannibalism of Objects* (1933).

Edward James's collection was broken up at a public sale, but many of the works are now to be found at the Boymans-Van Beuningen Museum in Rotterdam. From the James collection, London's Tate Modern owns the small painting *The Metamorphosis of Narcissus* (1937), as well as *The Cannibalism of Autumn*.

BIBLIOGRAPHY

Ades, Dawn, *Dalí*, London, 1982, rev. ed. 1995

Ades, Dawn, and Bradley, Fiona (eds.), *Salvador Dalí, A Mythology*, exhibition catalogue, Tate Gallery, Liverpool and Salvador Dalí Museum, Saint Petersburg, Florida, 1998–99

Ades, Dawn, Sutton, Peter C., and Zafran, Eric M. (eds.), *Dalí's Optical Illusions*, New Haven, 2000

Dalí, Salvador, *Diary of a Genius*, trans. Richard Howard, foreword and notes by Michel Déon, London, 1966

Dalí, Salvador, *The Secret Life of Salvador Dalí*, trans. Haakon M. Chevalier, New York, 1993 (1st edition: New York, 1942)

Dalí Architecture, exhibition catalogue, La Pedrera, Fundació Gala-Salvador Dalí and Fundació Caixa de Catalunya, Barcelona, 1996

Descharnes, Robert, *Salvador Dalí*, London and New York, 1985

Descharnes, Robert and Néret, Gilles, *Dalí: The Paintings*, Cologne and London, 1997

Finkelstein, Haim (ed.), *The Collected Writings of Salvador Dalí*, Cambridge, 1998

Finkelstein, Haim, *Salvador Dalí's Art and Writing, 1927–1942, The Metamorphoses of Narcissus*, Cambridge, 1996

Gaillemin, Jean-Louis, *Dalí, Désirs Inassouvis. Du Purisme au Surréalisme. 1925-1935*, Paris, 2002

Gibson, Ian, *Lorca-Dalí: El Amor Que No Pudo Ser*, Barcelona, 1999

Gibson, Ian, *The Shameful Life of Salvador Dalí*, London, 1997

Lubar, Robert S., *Dalí: The Salvador Dalí Museum Collection*, Boston and London, 2000
Raeburn, Michael (ed.), *Salvador Dalí: The Early Years*, exhibition catalogue, Hayward Gallery, London and Metropolitan Museum, New York, 1994
Salvador Dalí, Rétrospective 1920–1980, exhibition catalogue, Centre Georges-Pompidou, Paris, 1979

LIST OF ILLUSTRATIONS

The following abbreviations have been used:
a above; **b** below; **c** centre; **l** left; **r** right

COVER

Front *The Architectonic Angelus of Millet* (detail), oil on canvas, 73 × 60 cm, 1933. Museo Nacional Centro de Arte Reina Sofía, Madrid
Spine *Little Ashes* (detail), oil on wood, 64 × 48 cm, 1928. Museo Nacional Centro de Arte Reina Sofía, Madrid
Back *Impressions of Africa*, oil on canvas, 91.5 × 117.5 cm, 1938. Boymans-Van Beuningen Museum, Rotterdam

OPENING

1–9 *The First Days of Spring* (details; see p. 51), oil and collage on wood, 50 × 65 cm, 1929. The Salvador Dalí Museum, Saint Petersburg, Florida
11 *The Bust of a Retrospective Woman,* painted bronze, 70 × 54 × 35 cm. Private collection

CHAPTER 1

12 *Portrait of My Father*, oil on canvas, 90.5 × 66 cm, *c.* 1921. Fundació Gala-Salvador Dalí, Figueras
13 Dalí in 1921
14 The Dalí family at Es Llané, photograph. Fundació Gala-Salvador Dalí, Figueras
15 Dalí aged six, photograph. Fundació Gala-Salvador Dalí, Figueras
16 *View of Cadaqués*, oil on canvas, 29.2 × 48.3 cm, 1920. The Salvador Dalí Museum, Saint Petersburg, Florida
17 Cape Creus, photographs by Ian Gibson
18b *Trotsky*, ink and watercolour, 24 × 20.5 cm, *c.* 1923. Fundació Gala-Salvador Dalí, Figueras
18–19 *Self-Portrait with Raphaelesque Neck*, oil on canvas, 41.5 × 53 cm, 1920–21. Fundació Gala-Salvador Dalí, Figueras

CHAPTER 2

20 *Barcelonese Mannequin*, oil on canvas, 248 × 198 cm, 1927. Fundació Gala-Salvador Dalí, Figueras

21 Dalí and Lorca in 1925. Fundació Gala-Salvador Dalí, Figueras
22a Salvador Dalí's student card, 1924–25. Fundació Gala-Salvador Dalí, Figueras
22b Dalí's class at the Academy of San Fernando, Madrid in 1923, photograph. Fundació Gala-Salvador Dalí, Figueras
23 *Nightwalking Dreams,* watercolour on paper, 51.5 × 24 cm, 1922. Fundació Gala-Salvador Dalí, Figueras
24 *Still Life: Portrait of Federico García Lorca*, ink on paper, 16.3 × 22.4 cm, 1923. Fundació Gala-Salvador Dalí, Figueras
25l *Self-Portrait with L'Humanité*, oil and collage on cardboard, 104.9 × 75.4 cm, 1923. Fundació Gala-Salvador Dalí, Figueras
25r Salvador Dalí and Federico García Lorca at the students' residence, Madrid, 1922–23, photograph. Centre Georges-Pompidou, Paris
26 *Port Alguer*, oil on canvas, 99.5 × 98.5 cm, 1924. Fundació Gala-Salvador Dalí, Figueras
27b Federico García Lorca in front of *Still Life*, photograph. Centre Georges-Pompidou, Paris
27a *Still Life*, oil on canvas, 125 × 99 cm, 1924. Fundación Federico García Lorca, Madrid
28b Dalí and his sister Ana María in Cadaqués in 1925, photograph. Fundació Gala-Salvador Dalí, Figueras
28c *Self-Portrait*, drawing, published in *L'Amic de les Arts*, 31 January 1927
29 *Venus and Sailor, Homage to Salvat Passeit*, oil on canvas, 216 × 147 cm, 1925. Ikeda Museum of 20th-Century Art, Shizuoka
30 *Girl from the Back*, oil on canvas, 104 × 74 cm, 1925. Museo Nacional Centro de Arte Reina Sofía, Madrid
31 *Portrait of a Girl in a Landscape (Cadaqués)*, oil on canvas, 92 × 65 cm, *c.* 1926. Fundació Gala-Salvador Dalí, Figueras
32 *St Sebastian with the Head of a Sole*, drawing, 1927, published in *L'Amic de Les Arts*, 31 July 1927
33 *Neo-Cubist Academy (Composition with Three Figures)*, oil on canvas, 200 × 200 cm, 1926. Museu de Montserrat

34 *Apparatus and Hand*, oil on canvas, 62 × 47.5 cm, 1927. The Salvador Dalí Museum, Saint Petersburg

35 *The Spectral Cow*, oil on wood, 50 × 64.5 cm, 1928. Musée National d'Art Moderne, Centre Georges Pompidou, Paris

36 *Little Ashes*, oil on wood, 64 × 48 cm, 1928. Museo Nacional Centro de Arte Reina Sofía, Madrid

37 *Little Ashes*, details

38a *The Bather*, oil on board, 55.5 × 73.5 cm, 1928. The Salvador Dalí Museum, Saint Petersburg, Florida

38b *The Bather (Baigneuse)*, oil on panel, 63.5 × 75 cm, 1928. The Salvador Dalí Museum, Saint Petersburg, Florida

39a *The Bather*, 1928, detail

39b *The Bather (Baigneuse)*, detail

40a *Four Fishermen's Wives of Cadaqués*, oil on canvas, 147 × 196 cm, 1928. Museo Nacional Centro de Arte Reina Sofía, Madrid

40b *Anthropomorphic Beach*, oil, stone, sponge and wood, 47.5 × 27.7 cm, 1928. The Salvador Dalí Museum, Saint Petersburg, Florida

41 *Portrait of Luis Buñuel*, oil on canvas, 68.5 × 58.5 cm, 1924. Museo Nacional Centro de Arte Reina Sofía, Madrid

42b Scene from the film *Un Chien Andalou* by Luis Buñuel, 1929

42–43a Luis Buñuel and Salvador Dalí at Cape Creus in 1929. Fonds Luis Buñuel, Paris

43b Scene from the film *Un Chien Andalou* by Luis Buñuel, 1929

CHAPTER 3

44 *The Lugubrious Game*, oil and collage on cardboard, 44.4 × 30.3 cm, 1929. Private collection

45 Dalí in Cadaqués with superimposed image of Gala, photograph, 1934. Fundació Gala-Salvador Dalí, Figueras

46–47 *Ilumined Pleasures*, oil and collage on wood, 23.8 × 34.5 cm, 1929. The Museum of Modern Art, New York

48–49 *The Hand*, oil on canvas, 41 × 66 cm, 1930. The Salvador Dalí Museum, Saint Petersburg, Florida

49a Paul Eluard and André Breton, photograph by Man Ray

51a *The First Days of Spring*, oil and collage on wood, 50 × 65 cm, 1929. The Salvador Dalí Museum, Saint Petersburg, Florida

51b *The First Days of Spring*, detail

52 *Accommodations of Desire*, oil on wood, 22 × 35 cm, 1929. The Metropolitan Museum of Art, New York

53 The Paris Surrealists, photograph, 1930

54l *Portrait of Gala*, oil, ink and photograph on cardboard, 1931. Private collection

54b Dalí and Paul Eluard in 1929, photograph. Fundació Gala-Salvador Dalí, Figueras

55 *Portrait of Paul Eluard*, oil on cardboard, 33 × 25 cm, 1929. Private collection

56 Dalí in Cadaqués, summer 1931, photograph

57 Gala and Crevel in Cadaqués, summer 1931, photograph

58b *The Enigma of Desire, My Mother, My Mother, My Mother*, oil on canvas, 110 × 150.7 cm, 1929. Staatsgalerie moderner Kunst, Munich

58a *The Enigma of Desire, My Mother, My Mother, My Mother*, detail

59 Frontispiece of *Second Surrealist Manifesto*, watercolour, pencil and ink on paper, 30.5 × 26.7 cm, 1930

60a, b Scenes from the film *L'Age d'Or* by Luis Buñuel, 1930

61 *Profanation of the Host* and detail, oil on canvas, 100 × 73 cm, 1929. The Salvador Dalí Museum, Saint Petersburg, Florida

62 *Moment of Transition*, oil on canvas, 54 × 65 cm, 1934. Private collection

63 *Paranoiac Face*, retouched photographs, published in *Le Surréalisme au Service de la Révolution*, 1931

64 *William Tell*, oil and collage on canvas, 113 × 87 cm, 1930. Private collection

65 *The Font*, oil on canvas, 1930. The Salvador Dalí Museum, Saint Petersburg, Florida

66 *Solitude*, oil on canvas, 36 × 26 cm, 1931. Private collection

67 *Shades of Night Descending*, oil on canvas, 61 × 50 cm, 1931. The Salvador Dalí Museum, Saint Petersburg, Florida

69a *The Great Masturbator*, oil on canvas, 110 × 150 cm, 1929. Museo Nacional Centro de Arte Reina Sofía, Madrid

69b *The Persistence of Memory*, oil on canvas, 24 × 33 cm, 1931. The Museum of Modern Art, New York

CHAPTER 4

70 *The Spectre of Sex-Appeal*, oil on wood, 18 × 14 cm, 1934. Fundació Gala-Salvador Dalí, Figueras

71 Dalí, photograph, 1930

72–73 *Soft Skulls and Cranial Harp*, engraving, 37 × 30.5 cm, 1935. Brighton Museum and Art Gallery, Brighton

73 *Meditation on the Harp*, oil on canvas, 67 × 47 cm, 1932–34. The Salvador Dalí Museum, Saint Petersburg, Florida

74 *Soft Construction with Boiled Beans: Premonition of Civil War*, oil on canvas, 100 × 99 cm, 1936. Philadelphia Museum of Art, Philadelphia

75 *Burning Giraffe*, oil on wood, 35 × 27 cm, 1936–37. Kunstmuseum, Basel

76r *The Invisible Man*, oil on canvas, 143 × 81 cm, 1929–33. Museo Nacional Centro de Arte Reina Sofía, Madrid

76l *The Invisible Man*, detail

77 *The Weaning of Furniture-Nutrition*, oil on wood, 18 × 24 cm, 1934. The Salvador Dalí Museum, Saint Petersburg, Florida

78–79 *The Enigma of William Tell*, oil on canvas, 201.5 × 346 cm, 1933. Moderna Museet, Stockholm

80 *Invisible Sleeper, Horse, Lion*, oil on canvas, 50.2 × 65.2 cm, 1930. Musée National d'Art Moderne, Centre Georges Pompidou, Paris

81 *The Dream*, oil on canvas, 96 × 96 cm, 1931. The Cleveland Museum of Art

82 *The Great Paranoiac*, oil on canvas, 62 × 62 cm, 1936. Boymans-Van Beuningen Museum, Rotterdam

83 *Slave Market with Disappearing Bust of Voltaire*, oil on canvas, 46.5 × 65.5 cm, 1940. The Salvador Dalí Museum, Saint Petersburg, Florida

84–85b *Suburbs of the Paranoiac-Critical Town*, oil on wood, 46 × 66, 1936. Boymans-Van Beuningen Museum, Rotterdam

84–85a Studies for *Suburbs of the Paranoiac-Critical Town*, pencil and ink on paper, 32.5 × 20.3 cm, 1935. Private collection

86–87 *The Metamorphosis of Narcissus*, oil on canvas, 50.8 × 78.3 cm, 1937. Tate Gallery, London

89a, b Explanation of images in *The Endless Enigma*, from catalogue of Dalí exhibition at the Julien Levy Gallery, New York, 1939

89c *The Endless Enigma*, oil on canvas, 114.5 × 146.5 cm, 1938. Museo Nacional Centro de Arte Reina Sofía, Madrid

CHAPTER 5

90 *Portrait of Emilio Terry*, oil on wood, 34 × 27 cm, 1930. Private collection

91 Dalí in the garden of the Villa Marlia, photo by Anna-Laetitia Pecci-Blunt

92l The salon of the Hôtel Bischofsheim, owned by Charles and Marie-Laure de Noailles, decorated by Jean-Michel Frank, photograph by Roger Guillemot

92r The Noailles at the 'Bal des Matières', 1929

93 *The Old Age of William Tell*, oil on canvas, 98 × 140 cm, 1931. Private collection

94a Dalí at the Villa Marlia, photo by Anna-Laetitia Pecci-Blunt

94b Mae West's Lips Sofa, 86 × 182 × 80 cm, 1936. Private collection

95 Dalí and Anna-Laetitia Pecci-Blunt at the Villa Marlia

96 Anna Laetitia Pecci-Blunt and Emilio Terry at the Marcel Proust Ball at the home of the Prince and Princess de Faucigny-Lucinge. Private collection

97 Emilio Terry, the Princess de Faucigny-Lucinge and Jean Rouvier at the 'Bal des Matières' at the home of Charles and Marie-Laure de Noailles in 1929, photograph by G. L. Manuel frères. Private collection

98 *The Architectonic Angelus of Millet*, oil on canvas, 73 × 60 cm, 1933. Museo Nacional Centro de Arte Reina Sofía, Madrid

99 *Imperial Monument to the Child Woman*, oil on canvas, 140 × 80 cm, c. 1930. Museo Nacional Centro de Arte Reina Sofía, Madrid

100l *The City of Drawers*, study for *The Anthropomorphic Cabinet*, ink on paper, 32 × 41.5 cm. Private collection

100r *The Shoe (Surrealist Object Functioning Symbolically)*, shoe, modelling clay, milk glass, brush, sugar cubes, spoons, 48 × 24 × 14 cm, 1974. Private collection

101 *Cannibalism of Objects*, pencil, charcoal and chalk on Manila paper, 94 × 121 cm, 1932. Musée National d'Art Moderne, Centre Georges Pompidou, Paris

102 Set by Dalí for *Le Ballet du XXIe Siècle*, by Maurice Béjart, Théâtre des Champs-Elysées, Paris, 1962

103 Set by Dalí for the dream sequence of the film *Spellbound* by Alfred Hitchcock, 1945

104 *Venus with Drawers*, bronze, 98 × 32.5 × 34 cm, 1964. Fundació Gala-Salvador Dalí, Figueras

105 Gown by Schiaparelli using a motif by Dalí

106 *Lobster Telephone*, 1936, 30 × 15 × 17 cm. Boymans-Van Beuningen Museum, Rotterdam

106–107 Edward James and Igor Markevitch in the Tent Room at 35 Wimpole Street, London, in 1930, photograph by Norman Parkinson

107 *Chair with Long Arms*, sculpture. Private collection

108 Dalí arriving in New York in 1936

108–9 *Dream of Venus* Pavilion, New York, 1939

CHAPTER 6

110 *Soft Self-Portrait with Grilled Bacon*, oil on canvas, 61.3 × 50.8 cm, 1941. Private collection

111 Cover of *Time*, 14 December 1936
112 Dalí, Gala and Caresse Crosby at Hampton Manor in 1941, photo by Eric Schaal.
113 *Daddy Longlegs of the Evening...Hope!*, oil on canvas, 40.5 × 50.8 cm, 1940. The Salvador Dalí Museum, Saint Petersburg, Florida
114 *Galarina*, oil on canvas, 64.1 × 50.2 cm, 1944–45. Fundació Gala-Salvador Dalí, Figueras
115 *My Wife, Naked, Looking at her own Body, which is Transformed into Steps, Three Vertebrae of a Column, Sky and Architecture*, oil on wood, 61 × 52 cm, 1945. Private collection
116 *Leda Atomica*, oil on canvas, 61.1 × 45.3 cm, 1949. Fundació Gala-Salvador Dalí, Figueras
117 *The Dream of Christopher Columbus*, oil on canvas, 410 × 284 cm, 1958–59. The Salvador Dalí Museum, Saint Petersburg, Florida
118 *Christ of St John of the Cross*, oil on canvas, 205 × 116 cm, 1951. Art Gallery and Museum, Glasgow
119 *The Madonna of Port Lligat*, oil on canvas, 48.9 × 37.5 cm, 1949. Marquette University Fine Art Committee, Milwaukee
120a *Rhinocerotic Disintegration of Illissus of Phidias*, oil on canvas, 100 × 129.5 cm, 1954.

Fundació Gala-Salvador Dalí, Figueras
120b Dalí and a rhinoceros, photograph by Philippe Halsman
121 *Exploding Raphaelesque Head*, oil on canvas, 43 × 33 cm, 1951. Private collection.
122–23 *Tunny Fishing*, oil on canvas, 304 × 404 cm, 1966–67. Fondation Paul Ricard, Paris
125 *Hallucinogenic Toreador*, oil on canvas, 400 × 300 cm, 1969–70. The Salvador Dalí Museum, Saint Petersburg, Florida
126 Avida Dollars, photograph by Philippe Halsman
127 *Perpignan Station*, oil on canvas, 295 × 406 cm, 1965. Museum Ludwig, Cologne
128 *Young Virgin Auto-Sodomized by Her Own Chastity*, oil on canvas, 40.5 × 30.5 cm, 1954. Private collection
129 *Furniture-personage*, sketch, ink, 18.3 × 15.5 cm, 1934. Kunsthalle, Hamburg

DOCUMENTS

137 Breton, Dalí and Crevel in Stockholm, 1935
143 Buñuel, Dalí and Ana María in Figueras, 1929

INDEX OF WORKS

A

Accommodations of Desire 42, 49, 52–53, 58
Anthropomorphic Beach 40
Apparatus and Hand 34–35, 39, 46
Apparition of Face and Fruit Dish on a Beach 82
Architectonic Angelus of Millet, The 98, 101
Assumpta Corpuscularia Lapislazulina 117
Atavistic Remains After the Rain 101

B

Barcelonese Mannequin 20
Bather, The 38–39
Bather (Baigneuse) 38–39

Battle of Tetuan, The 117
Burning Giraffe 75

C

Cannibalism of Objects 101
Christ of St John of the Cross 118
City of Drawers, The 100
Composition with Three Figures 33
Corpus Hypercubicus 117
Couple with Heads Full of Clouds 106
Creation of Monsters, The 106

D–E

Daddy Longlegs of the Evening...Hope! 113–14
Dream, The 81

Dream of Christopher Colombus, The 117
Endless Enigma, The 83, 88–89, 112
Enigma of Desire, The 58, 93
Enigma of William Tell, The 78–79
Exploding Raphaelesque Head 119, 121

F

First Days of Spring, The 50–51, 83, 100
Font, The 65
Forest of Apparatus, The 34, 46
Four Fishermen's Wives of Cadaqués 40

G

Galarina 114, 117
Girl from the Back 29–30

Girl Standing at the Window 28
Great Masturbator, The 68–69, 100
Great Paranoiac, The 82, 106, 121

H

Hallucinogenic Toreador 121, 125
Hand, The 48–49

I

Illumined Pleasures 42, 46–47
Imperial Monument to the Child Woman 99–100
Impressions of Africa 106
Invisible Afghan with Apparition of García Lorca's Face on the Beach in the Form of a

Fruit Bowl with Three Figs 55
Invisible Man, The 55, 68, 76, 93
Invisible Sleeper, Horse, Lion 80, 93

L–M

Leda Atomica 116–17
Little Ashes 34, 36–37, 39, 46
Lugubrious Game, The 44, 52, 58, 60, 93, 100
Madonna of Port Lligat 117, 119
Meditation on the Harp 73
Metamorphosis of Narcissus 83, 85–87, 112
Moment of Transition 62
My Wife, Naked, Looking at Her Own Body, which is Transformed into Steps, Three Vertebrae of a Column, Sky and Architecture 114–15

N–O

Nightwalking Dreams 23
Old Age of William Tell, The 93

P

Paranoiac Face 63
Perpignan Station 127
Persistence of Memory, The 68–69
Port Alguer 26, 28
Portrait of a Girl in a Landscape 28, 31
Portrait of Emilio Terry 73, 90
Portrait of Federico García Lorca 24
Portrait of Gala 54
Portrait of Luis Buñuel 41
Portrait of Marie-Laure de Noailles 93
Portrait of My Father 12
Portrait of Paul Eluard 54–55, 58
Profanation of the Host 61, 100

Purist Still Life 27
Putrefied Donkey, The 35

R

Rhinocerotic Disintegration of Illisus of Phidias 120

S

Saint Sebastian with the Head of a Sole 32
Santiago el Grande 117, 119
Self-Portrait with L'Humanité 25
Self-Portrait with Raphaelesque Neck 18–19
Shades of Night Descending 67
Slave Market with Disappearing Bust of Voltaire 83
Sleep 106
Soft Construction with Boiled Beans 74
Soft Self-Portrait with Grilled Bacon 110–11

Soft Skulls and Cranial Harp 72
Solitude 66
Spain 106
Spectral Cow, The 35
Spectre of Sex Appeal, The 70–71
Still Life 27
Suburbs of the Paranoiac-Critical Town 81, 84–85, 88

T–Z

Trotsky 18
Tunny Fishing 121–23
Unsatisfied Desires 35
Venus and Sailor 28–29
Venus with Drawers 105
View of Cadaqués 16
Weaning of Furniture-Nutrition, The 77
White Calm 106
William Tell 43, 49, 64
Woman's Head in the Form of a Battle 82
Young Virgin Auto-Sodomized by her Own Chastity 128

INDEX

A

Age d'Or, L' 59–61, 92–93
Alexandre, Maxime 77
Aragon, Louis 22, 77, 95
Arcimboldo, Giuseppe 82, 88, 112
Arp, Jean (Hans) 50, 53
Auric, Georges 95

B

Balanchine, George 105
Balzac, Honoré de 124
Barr, Alfred 107
Bataille, Georges 58, 59, 77, 80, 102
Batcheff, Pierre 121
Bea, Isidor 117, 119

Beaton, Cecil 104
Beaumont, Etienne de 92, 105
Béjart, Maurice 102
Bello, Pepín 23, 40
Bérard, Christian 42, 68, 94–95, 105–6
Berman brothers 68
Berman, Eugène 105
Böcklin, Arnold 99, 105
Bosch, Hieronymus 29
Botticelli, Sandro 108
Bracelli, Giovanni Battista 105, 112
Bramante, Donato 113–15
Brassaï 98
Breton, André 19, 46–49, 53, 58–59, 62–63, 76–80, 91, 93, 102, 107–8, 114, 117

Bucher, Jeanne 93
Buñuel, Luis 21, 23, 29, 35, 40–43, 54, 59–60

C

Calas, Nicolas 112
Carrà, Carlo 27
Casson, Hugh 106
Chanel, Coco 104–5
Cheval, Facteur 107
Chien Andalou, Un 21, 41–43, 46, 48–49, 59, 93, 102, 121
Chirico, Giorgio de 27, 32, 37, 47, 68, 93, 121
Cocteau, Jean 42
Cosimo, Piero di 112
Crevel, René 53, 55, 80, 93, 102, 121

Crosby, Caresse 94, 112, 114
Cuevas de Vera, Margaret (Tota) 94

D

Dalí, Ana María 14, 21, 28–29
Dalí, Gal 85
Dalí, Gala *see* Gala
Dalmau Gallery 19, 21, 26
Degas, Edgar 18
Derain, André 105
Disney, Walt 103
Documents 58, 62
Domènech, Anselm 15, 18
Durst, André 94, 104

E

Einstein, Albert 22
Einstein, Carl 62
Eluard, Gala *see* Gala
Eluard, Paul 49–50,
52–55, 77, 93
Ernst, Max 47, 50, 53,
93, 95, 103, 107
Esprit Nouveau, L' 18

F

Fanes, Felix 126
Faucigny-Lucinge,
Prince de 94–95
Faucigny-Lucinge, Baba
d'Erlanger, Princess de
94–95, 105
Finkelstein, Haim 126
Francesca, Piero della
119
Frank, Jean-Michel
92–93, 95
Freud, Sigmund 47,
52, 65, 98, 112, 114

G

Gala 45, 49, 52–55,
58, 60, 68, 71, 76, 79,
85, 88, 93, 95, 102,
106–9, 111, 114–17,
124, 126–27
García Lorca, Federico
21, 24–29, 32–35,
40–42, 46, 121, 124,
126
Gasch, Sebastià 46
Gaudí, Antoni 13,
15–16, 98, 107
Giacometti, Alberto
93, 95
Giacometti, Diego 95
Gibson, Ian 18, 26, 82,
121, 126
Goemans, Camille
49–50, 58–60
Goethe, Johann
Wolfgang von 112
Gómez de la Serna,
Ramón 23
Gorsen, Peter 126
Grandville, Jean Gérard
105
Green, Anne 94

Green, Julien 94
Gris, Juan 24, 27, 121
Guimard, Paul 98, 107

H

Halsman, Philippe 114,
120, 126
Hartford, Huntington
117
Hitchcock, Alfred
103–4
Hitler, Adolf 77–78
Holbein, Hans 73
Horst, Horst P. 108–9
Hugo, Jean 95
Hugo, Valentine 102
Humanité, L' 24

J–K

Jacob, Max 22, 95
James, Edward 103,
105–8
Keaton, Buster 32, 42

L

Lacan, Jacques 71–72,
81, 88
Langdon, Harry 41
Laporte, René 94
Lautréamont, Comte de
26, 37, 75, 104, 124
Le Corbusier 27, 32,
42, 98, 115
Ledoux, Claude-Nicolas
95
Léger, Fernand 42
Leiris, Michel 58
Lenin 78
Leo XIII, Pope 95
L'Espée, Baron de 95
Levy, Julien (Gallery)
88, 108–9, 111–12
Limbour, Georges 58
Loeb, Pierre 46

M

Magritte, René 50
Mallo, Maruja 23
Manet, Edouard 18
Manso, Margarita 29,
32
Mantegna, Andrea 118

Marinetti, Filippo
Tommaso 23
Markevitch, Igor 106
Marx Brothers 104
Massine, Léonide 105
Masson, André 46, 53
Menjou, Adolphe 41
Millet, Jean-François
71, 74, 98, 101
Minotaure 72, 98, 101,
107
Miró, Joan 46, 48–49,
93–94, 112
Momper, Josse de 82
Morand, Paul 95
Morandi, Giorgio 24,
27, 32

N

*New Limits of Painting,
The* 46
Nietzsche, Friedrich
105
Nin, Anaïs 114
Noailles, Charles de 42,
58, 60, 92–95
Noailles, Marie-Laure
Bischofsheim 92–95,
105

O

Olivier, Fernande 16
Ortiz, Manuel Angel
29
Ozenfant, Amédée 27

P–Q

Pacioli, Luca 119
Palladio, Andrea 95
Parkinson, Norman
106
Pecci-Blunt, Anna-
Laetitia (Mimi),
Countess 91, 94–95
Peck, Gregory 103
Pérez Barradas, Rafael
23
Petit, François 101
Pevsner, Nikolaus 98
Picabia, Francis 19
Picasso, Pablo 14, 16,
23, 29, 42, 50, 63, 93,
106

Pichot, Pepito 14, 16,
18
Pichot, Ramón 14, 18
Piranesi, Giovanni
Battista 95
Platt-Lynes, George
108
Poulenc, Francis 95
Proust, Marcel 95
Publicitat, La 24, 48

R

Radiguet, Raymond 93
Rank, Otto 98
Raphael 19, 113
Ratton, Charles 105
Ray, Man 32, 41–42,
50, 53, 98, 111
Redon, Odilon 32
Renoir, Auguste 18
Revista de Occidente
29
*Révolution Surréaliste,
La* 42, 46, 58
Ricard, Paul 123
Rimbaud, Arthur 45,
49, 58–59
Rivera, Primo de 22,
25
Roger, Carme 18
Rolo, Felix 94
Romains, Jules 80
Romero, Luis 121, 124
Rouvier, Jean 95

S

Sade, Laure de 92
Sade, Marquis de
62–63
Sadoul, Georges 77
Saint-Jean, Robert de
94
Santos Torroella, Rafael
126
Sardou, Victorien 107
Schiaparelli, Elsa
104–5
Schwitters, Kurt 107
Sert, José Maria 85
Solimena, Francesco 93
Stendhal 115
*Surréalisme au Service de
la Révolution, Le*
60, 63, 76, 102

Surréalisme et la Peinture, Le 46
Surrealist Manifesto 46, 58–59

T

Tanguy, Yves 46, 53, 93
Tchelitchew, Pavel 105–6

Tcherina, Ludmila 102
Teilhard de Chardin, Pierre 121
Terry, Emilio 73, 91, 94–95, 100, 105–7
Torre, Guillermo de 23
Trotsky, Leon 18–19
Tzara, Tristan 23, 42, 53

U–V

Unik, Pierre 77
Valéry, Paul 22
Valori Plastici 18, 26
Verlaine, Paul 23, 59
Vermeer, Johannes 29, 74, 119
Vinci, Leonardo da 82, 88, 100, 112, 117
Vitruvius 121

W

Wagner, Richard 105
Wells, H. G. 22
West, Mae 95, 107
Wildenstein, Georges 58, 103

PICTURE CREDITS

AKG Paris 78–79, 118, 127. Beetmann/Corbis 108a. Bridgeman Giraudon, Paris back cover, 11, 29, 35, 36–37, 44, 55, 58, 62, 66, 69b, 70, 75, 81, 82, 83, 84–85, 94b, 98, 100l, 106l, 107r, 115, 116, 117, 119, 121, 128, 129. Bridgeman Giraudon/Charmet, Paris 53. Brighton Art Gallery 72–73. CNAC/MNAM Dist. RMN, Paris 80, 101. Collection Christophe L., Paris 42b, 43b, 60a, 60b. Connaissances des Arts, Paris 92l. Fond Luis Buñuel, Paris 42–43, 143. Fundació Gala-Salvador Dalí, Figueras 12, 14, 15, 18b, 20, 21, 22, 23, 24, 25l, 26, 28bl, 40a, 45, 54r, 76, 100r, 104, 114. Ian Gibson 17. Halsman Philippe/Magnum Photos 120b, 126. Hulton-Deutsch Collection/Corbis 71. Keystone, Paris 102. Leemage, Paris 137. Man Ray Trust/ADAGP, Paris 2002 49a. MNAM/CCI Archive, Paris 25r, 27l, 56, 57, 64, 91, 94, 95, 108–109.Museu de Montserrat 33. Norman Parkinson Ltd/Fiona Cowan, Londres 106-107. Oronoz, Madrid front cover, spine, 18–19, 27r, 30, 31, 41, 54l, 69a, 74, 89, 99, 110, 120a, 122–123, 125. Photos 12.Com/ARJ 93. Rue des Archives, Paris 13. Sotheby's Picture Library, London 90. Tate Picture Library, London 86–87. Telimages, Paris 49a. The Metropolitan Museum of Art, New York 52, 102–103. The Museum of Modern Art, New York 46–47. The Salvador Dalí Museum, Saint Petersburg 1, 2–3, 4–5, 6–7, 8–9, 16, 34, 38–39, 40b, 48–49, 51, 61, 65, 67, 73, 77, 113. Timepix 111, 112.

ACKNOWLEDGMENTS

I would like to thank Elisabeth de Farcy with whom I discussed the idea of this book in the Jardin des Tuileries and who kept it in mind, and also Daniel Abadie for his thoughts on Dalí as well as the late Patrice Bachelard, Frédéric Morvan and Anne Soto, Chloé Boyeldieu, Natalie Mennasseyre, Felix Fanes and Montse Aguer. Thanks also go to my director of studies at the Université Paris IV- Sorbonne, Bruno Foucart, as well as my thesis reviewers, whose comments and advice were extremely useful: José Vovelle, Thierry Dufrêne and Serge Lemoine. Thanks also to Marie-Claude Beaud, Alain Beausire, Stella Beddoe, Claude Bernard, Gérard Benoit Alexandre Biaggi, David Biggelman, Christian Boutonnet, Guy Boyer, Joanne Bremner, Antoine Broccardo, Steven Calloway, Jean-Loup Champion, Martin Chapman, the late Stephane Deschamp, Marc Dessauce, Philippe Duboÿ, Anne-Sophie Duval, Jean Fournier, Philip Garner, Marie-Noël de Gary, Yves Gastou, Ian Gibson, Didier Girard, Adrien Goetz, Alvar Gonzalès-Palacios, Maïté Hudry, Barthélemy Jobert, Philip Jodidio, Sandrine Lalau, Elisabeth Lebovici, James Lord, Benjamin Loyauté, Alain Mérot, Monique Mosser, Raphaël Ortiz, Costi Papachristopoulos, Annie Pérez, Alexandre Pradère, Raphaël Sadouki, Béatrice Salmon, Josiane Sartre, Helmuth D. Stöcker, Ingrid Strömberg and Maud Traon. Special thanks to Doryck Sembaz for your wit and good humour.

Jean-Louis Gaillemin
teaches history of contemporary art at the Université
Paris IV- Sorbonne. He has worked as a writer and editor
for art magazines both in France and internationally,
and is the author of several books.

Translated from the French by David H. Wilson

First published in the United Kingdom in 2004 by
Thames & Hudson Ltd, 181A High Holborn,
London WC1V 7QX

British Library Cataloguing-in-Publication Data

A catalogue record for this book is available
from the British Library

ISBN 0–500–30115–8

Printed and bound in Italy by Editoriale Lloyd, Trieste